Best
Website®

Simple Steps to Successful Websites

Nelson Bates

BookSurge Publishing
Published 2008 United States of America

For additional copies please visit BestWebsite.com

All rights reserved,
Copyright © Nelson Bates 2008

ISBN 1-4196-9000-0
ISBN-13 9781419690006
Library of Congress Control Number 2008902072

The *Best Website* book is protected under United States copyright laws, among others being 17 U.S.C. Sec 102(a).
No portion of this book may be reproduced or distributed without the expressed written consent of the owner.

Additionally, any electronic retrieval and recovery system used to store and disseminate this text and/or images is prohibited.

Bates, Nelson

Library of Congress
Copyright Office
101 Independence Avenue, S.E.
Washington, DC 20559-6000

1 2 3 4 5 6 7 8 9 10

Table of Contents...

*To my Mom, who inspires me and encourages me
every day, in business and in life..*

Thanks Mom!!...

So why listen to me?

I have been making money online since 1995. Most recently, I built from scratch BuySellWebsite.com into the Internet's most popular marketplace for buying and selling website businesses.

This business was chosen by the #1 Internet marketing company in the world, *The Internet Marketing Center®*, as a Featured Success Story.

I also developed the Internet's longest running Website Appraisal ™ system that was sold through BuySellWebsite.com. This allowed me to learn how hundreds of other website owners had made their businesses successful.

I have also had the opportunity to work as a Web Master for Walt Disney World®, where I learned how to design websites from some of the most talented web designers in the world.

➤ And I have great news for you! There are more ways to make money online than ever before. I will show you the Fastest, Most Reliable way to build a **remarkably profitable website business!**

Introduction

Many times successful business owners write books to show what they've done to be successful. For the most part, this is a great way to obtain excellent advice. Both Robert Kiyosaki and Donald Trump fall into this category.

Kiyosaki has sold more than 26 million books through his **Rich Dad, Poor Dad** investment series. And Trump has had numerous *New York Times* best-selling books.

It is interesting to note, however, that when business owners reach this level, they tend to give advice in general, broad strokes about the "way" to success.

This approach is evident in their latest book, written together, **Why We Want You to Be Rich.** The authors state in their introduction that "this is not a how-to book." This leaves the reader not knowing the specifics of **how** to build a successful business.

It is not my intention to discount the advice given by these two businessmen. Both are helpful and inspiring. I am only saying that I provide the specific advice that they do not.

The book you are reading now **is** a "How-To" book. It contains all the specific steps and strategies of how to build a successful Internet business that can earn hundreds of thousands of dollars per year, if not millions. In the pages that follow, I will show you how to build the **Best Website**™ possible!

Two Main Points to Making Money Online

1. The most important aspect of making money online

is also the hardest thing to do. This is creating significant and consistent traffic to your website. To illustrate why traffic is the most important aspect, consider this: when I was running my website appraisal business, we received submissions from some of the most poorly designed websites that were earning $10,000 to $20,000+ per month in profit. The key was that they had a tremendous flow of traffic.

I never saw a single example of a great looking website, with no or low traffic, making lots of money. I did, however, see plenty of bad and mediocre websites making incredible money, simply because they had excellent traffic.

2. The second main point to making money online is designing a great website. This is split into two parts:

    a. Part one is the modifications you make to your website to optimize it for the Search Engines.

    b. Part two is everything else that makes up your website, like graphics, layout, navigation structure, and the sales process.

In the design of your website, you want to create immediate credibility in the eyes of the potential customers and effectively lead them through your website to make a purchase (i.e., the sales process), thus, maximizing the number of buyers you get in relation to the number of visitors you receive.

Also, the people who make the most money online, at the very least, know how either to manage their own website (e.g., being able to update content, add links and graphics), or to build the entire website themselves from scratch using one of the professional design tools like Adobe DreamWeaver or Microsoft Expression Web. There are certainly exceptions to this rule but, in general, this is true.

Knowing how to manage and/or build your own website allows all your ideas to come to life without having to pay a web designer (who usually can't ever quite deliver what you intended anyway!).

By learning the methods I show in this book, you will be able to dramatically enhance your ability to manage or build your own website in a fraction of the time and with far better results than trying to pay a designer to build your site.

Don't worry if you've never done this before or have tried in the past and felt overwhelmed; I'll show you a number of ways to get things done effectively either entirely by yourself or by hiring out the details that you don't feel comfortable doing yourself. Some of the tasks you may wish to outsource are: database design, Flash creation and graphic design, to name a few.

So why do most people lose money online?

I believe people lose money online for two reasons. The first reason is because they get bogged down in the details of building their business. Things like server platforms, coding choices, graphic design, layout options, entity formation, and search engine optimization, among others. **It's very easy to get confused and lose track of where you need to go.**

The second reason is that they don't allow enough time for their business to succeed. Most people will not continue past three months if their business does not start to make money. They become frustrated with the process and give up.

In my opinion, you'll need at least 3 to 6 months to establish a solid website and start generating enough traffic to become profitable. It just takes that long to refine your website and gain search engine traffic. But, as long as you know what the right path is, you'll know to keep going.

Ok, let's get started …

CH. 1 **The BestWebsite® Essential 9**™

The BestWebsite Essential 9™ - The nine most important things you can do now to make your website a profitable success:

1.) **Create a Remarkable Aspect to Your Website**

... It is far less expensive to build a remarkable website than it is to advertise an average one. Come up with a remarkable aspect for your product, service, business etc., then incorporate it into your website. Give people a **reason** to talk about your website and they will do your promotion for you!! (20-40hrs, $500 varies widely)

2.) **Proper Keyword Research ...** Use *WordTracker.com* and *Google Suggest* to select the proper keywords and begin search engine optimization on your website. (10-15hrs, $59)

3.) **Setup a Free Squidoo.com Page ...** This is an excellent way to boost your search engine rankings by creating links from your *Squidoo* page back to your website. It is also an excellent way to generate valuable traffic from the *Squidoo* community. (2-5hrs, FREE)

4.) **Create Articles that Provide Useful Information**
...
Start by creating three or four articles that provide useful information related to your product or service, then post them on your website and target the keywords you selected earlier. (5-10hrs, FREE)

5.) **Digg, Del.icio.us and StumbleUpon your Articles**
... Use these free services to let the world know about your articles. These services also provide a dramatic boost in your search rankings. (2-4hrs, FREE)

6.) Purchase a <u>Yahoo Directory Listing</u> ... This is a great way to get a link from the #1 website in the world to your website. A Yahoo employee reviews your website, categorizes it and then places a link to you. Both Yahoo and Google check if you have this link and boost your search engine rankings. (1hr, $299/yr)

7.) Press Release with <u>PRWeb</u> and <u>Majon</u> ... This is a fantastic way to be able to choose keywords in your press release that are posted on their top ranked websites that link back to yours. Not only do they significantly enhance your search engine rankings, they also announce your business and products to the media. (3-5hrs, $308)

8.) Laser Targeted Purchased Advertising ... Find top websites in your industry and purchase advertising from them. This may be one of the best methods of gaining substantial traffic. Not only do you get traffic from the websites you advertise on, but you can also drastically increase your search engine rankings because important websites in your industry are linking to you. (20hrs research, $100 and up)

9.) Google Analytics and Yahoo Search Submit ...
The more the search engines know about you, the better. Don't make them guess. By installing *Google Analytics* on your web pages and submitting your website to *Yahoo Search Submit*, you let them gain valuable knowledge about your website and, in turn, they will rank you better! (5-10hrs, Google FREE, Yahoo $59/yr)

Approximate total time and money spent low end --- **68 hours, $1,325**
Approximate total time and money spent high end --- **110 hours, $3,525+**

*Check www.BestWebsite.com/The-Essential-9.htm for updates and to follow the above hyperlinks.

CH. 2 What Type of Website to Start

I want first to mention the structure of a successful website. I'll define a successful website as **the website that makes the most money, takes the least amount of time to run, and provides the most flexibility**. The most successful website structure I have encountered is managed by a single owner who hires out some of the duties of his or her website business, like graphic design and database design, and then manages the Internet marketing campaign and any website updates alone.

There are certainly many ways to build a successful website. For instance, if you have the Internet marketing knowledge, and someone else has the website design knowledge, you can partner to build a great website. Of course, this means you lose some control, and you have to split your profits. I will show in Chapter 4 how to get all the work done by either doing it yourself or hiring it out.

Deciding what "type" of product to sell is pretty simple. **You'll have the best opportunity of making the most money with a product to which you own the rights,** whether it is a physical product, an information product, or a service.

If you have a product that can be delivered completely online, preferably without your involvement, this is probably your best bet at making a consistent and significant profit online.

I'd like to use BuySellWebsite.com as a great example of a service product. Among other things, BuySellWebsite.com sold classified ad listings to people wanting to sell their website businesses. The classified listings we sold were $99 and cost essentially nothing to provide. Whether we sold one or one thousand, it still cost the same small amount of time and money. Note: I have since sold BuySellWebsite.com

> **Tip:** In Chapter 4, I will show you how I built the classified ad database from scratch with no programming knowledge.

The classified ad listing is a great example of a product that can be delivered online. If you have a product or service that is delivered online without your involvement, your profit margin will be much greater than with a traditional product. You'll see, later on, that you'll probably need this extra profit margin and any extra time to survive the startup process and pay for your marketing campaign.

By choosing a product that is delivered online, you are starting out on the right foot. I don't want to make it sound like you cannot succeed with a traditional physical product. I'm just saying that, in general, on online product is probably the most effective and profitable option.

A few more examples of products delivered online are e-books or membership sites where users pay a monthly fee to access information. Another example is Website Appraisals. This is a service that we sold on BuySellWebsite.com and the appraisals were then delivered through e-mail in an Adobe PDF document.

Databases: Your Hardest Working Employee

Let's look further into the BuySellWebsite.com classified ad as an example of a service delivered online without the owner's involvement.

When a person wanted to place a classified ad, they clicked on a payment button to start the process. We used PayPal as our merchant account provider (more on PayPal later). Once payment was made through PayPal, they were redirected back to our site where they could fill out the ad listing form that was then automatically uploaded to the site and rotated into the active listings through the database I created.

The database also allowed users to retrieve lost passwords, delete old ads, update their listings and track how many times each ad was viewed. A database can be your best friend and hardest working employee. It might sound like a complicated process to set up, and it can be, but I built it entirely by myself using my web design software's Database Wizards. (I use Microsoft Expression Web; there will be more on web design software in Chapter 4.)

What does this mean? It means I built the entire database by going through a 'wizard' that asked me questions about how I wanted my database to operate, then Expression Web wrote the database code for me! This is an incredibly powerful tool. By learning the Database Wizard, you can eliminate having to pay for a database designer.

Virtually all people who work with Web developers find the process very expensive and incredibly difficult to get what they want. Most people fail to make it beyond trying to design their site because it becomes too difficult to continually explain what they want and then they run out of money. **The more you are in control of your website, the better off you'll be**.

Affiliate Programs as a Revenue Stream

Along the lines of effortless income, there is one revenue stream I did want to mention as something to stay away from. While it can be beneficial to advertise affiliate programs as <u>part</u> of your website, I don't recommend building your business around them. If you base your business on promoting someone else's product, you are at the mercy of changing payouts, percentages, cut off levels, minimums and any other changes that may unexpectedly come up. Not to mention the fact that the commissions are almost always too low ever to turn a profit, let alone a consistent one you can live on.

It's okay to advertise affiliate programs as <u>part</u> of your website, just don't build your business around it.

Success Means a Profitable Website

I've written this book from the standpoint of describing what I've found to be successful with notes as to why it was successful. I will also list the things that other website owners have found to be successful. After you have read the steps I describe to building a successful website, you'll be able to apply it to your situation.

The point of this book is to help you get your Internet business past the start up phase, in other words, to bring the business to the point of breaking even … and then to move on to creating $10,000 a month and more in profit. So few people make it past the breakeven point, and I want to make sure we get you past this; I apologize if I bore some of the more advanced Netpreneurs but, hopefully, you will consider it a good review and will learn a few things along the way too.

In almost any sport, the players and coaches on a team that has won in the past know how to win in the future. It is a huge advantage to "know" what it takes to win. You know what things to focus on, what things to ignore and how to pace yourself.

The same holds true for business success. I have been through the complete process of building an Internet company from scratch into something very successful many times over. I have also had the opportunity to review hundreds of others who have done it by performing Website Appraisals for some of the Internet's most successful websites.

If you haven't yet built a successful website or are stuck with a website that is only marginally profitable and don't know how to turn it into a very successful business, I hope you'll take this unique opportunity to learn from my experience. When I was starting out, I had no spare money and limited knowledge about building websites and Internet marketing. I really had no idea it was going to be as incredibly difficult, time consuming and expensive as it turned out to be.

But the good news is that, from all that I have learned, I intend to show you some tremendous shortcuts and amazing tips and tricks to building your own highly successful website with a fraction of the time, effort and expense!

Note: One of the most difficult things to describe is how to know when to move on from a particular task. For instance, when is your website good enough to start working on Internet marketing? Or the reverse, when do you have enough traffic and need to come back to and improve your website's sales process and conversion rate?

Profitable Doesn't Require Perfection!

Whether it is dealing with web design, database design or Internet marketing, the key is not to try to make things 100% right. This might sound like bad advice at first. But because there are so many things the owner of a successful website must do well to consistently make money online, those making the most money online know when to move on from a particular task. I explain the specifics of this advice throughout the book.

CH. 3 Before You Start Designing Your Website

Most people who start an online business will spend far too much time just getting things set up and won't have enough time or money to spend on the things that will actually make him or her money.

This chapter is set up to get past many of the start up issues as quickly as possible, so you can focus on creating additional traffic to your website and improving your sales process.

Okay, let's get started!

If I were starting an Internet business now, these are the things I would need to accomplish. In no particular order …

1. The Name of the Business

2. Domain Name

3. Website Server

4. Form an LLC or Inc.

5. Trademark Registration

6. Misc. things, like business cards

The Name of Your Business.

In most situations I recommend the name of the business be the same as the domain name. It makes things much easier in general, as you'll see below.

There are two schools of thought here: go with a keyword generated name or go with a name you make up. My preference is to go with a keyword-generated name because it's easier to target the search engines and it's more recognizable in marketing campaigns that have the URL listed in it.

Examples of keyword-generated names are BuySellWebsite. com or BabyCribs.com and examples of made up names are Yahoo.com or Digg.com.

As another example, when I chose BestWebsite as the name of this business, I registered the domain name BestWebsite. com, then formed an LLC in its name (BestWebsite, LLC) and filed the Federal Trademark "BestWebsite." I also opened a Bank account in its name and set up a PayPal account in its name. The name also serves as my email account moreinfo@ bestwebsite.com.

I think this is important because when people come to my site they like to see that the domain name is the same as the LLC name and when they make a payment they like seeing that the payment is going to the same business name as everything else.

Creating credibility with your website is certainly the most important thing when convincing people to do business with you. The little things do matter. And it is definitely worth it to expend the effort to set your business up this way.

Domain Name

In general, you should try for a two or three word domain name that contains the keywords of your industry. An excellent way to discover the best keywords for your industry is by using the keyword service by WordTracker.com They do a great job of showing which keywords are the most searched for and least competitive, giving you the best chance of success.

More often than not, the most searched for keywords in your industry will already have the domain name registered. However, as an example, if you really wanted BabyCribs.com, you could register myBabyCribs.com or BabyCribsHome.com. (Before you select a name, read the Trademark section in this chapter.)

Having an excellent domain name will definitely make things easier when it comes to search engine optimization and creating credibility when people visit your site. For instance, the domain name BestWebsite.com had already been registered to someone else before I negotiated to buy it. I knew it was exactly the name I wanted and was willing to pay a premium for it.

You can find lots of premium domains for sale at SEDO.com or GreatDomains.com. If you are just starting out, however, I recommend going to GoDaddy.com and registering a domain name as close as you can get to your keywords. That way you only end up paying nine dollars for your domain name, instead of possibly thousands of dollars for a premium domain name.

It's difficult to make a recommendation of what exactly to do without seeing your situation. But a name is very important and carefully choosing the best name for your business is important. As a general rule-of-thumb, don't spend more than 10% of your budget on it. You'll probably need every dollar you've got to make sure you get through the start up process. You can rethink the name when you're profitable. That might sound crazy, but businesses do it all the time.

For instance, here is another example of choosing a domain name. A friend of mine is building her photography website to sell her photography services. She has decided to use her own name, Sarah Martini, as the name of the business, Sarah Martini, LLC and the domain name is SarahMartini.com. This arrangement is fine and works well for this situation.

My goal from here on out is to make sure you make it through the start up phase. To me, the start up phase lasts until the website can earn enough money to operate without any outside money being put in. Only a very small number of people make it past this phase and I hope I can help you through it.

Note: Be aware that when you are registering a domain name with GoDaddy.com, they will try to sell you a bunch of add-on services, like hosting, advertising and an anonymous listing to name a few. I don't recommend purchasing anything else from them. Also, there are certainly many other places on the Internet to register your domain name, such as NetworkSolutions.com and TuCows.com, I just have a preference for GoDaddy.com.

Website Server

I've used many different Web servers to host my websites over the years, and there is one clear winner that is the best in every category. It is Intermedia.net. I've discovered that no matter how big, small, or complicated your site or how many visitors you get to your site, Intermedia.net can handle almost every situation. They have hosting packages that will fit most people's needs, handling virtually any script you can think of to run on it, for $15.95 per month.

Please note: I do NOT receive compensation from any of the websites I recommend in this book. I will disclose compensation information if there is an exception.

They also offer a very user-friendly control panel that lets you manage your server via any Web browser. They make setting up e-mail accounts and filtering spam very easy. They also include, at no additional cost, an excellent website statistics tracking software that allows you to see who is visiting your site, where they are coming from, how long they are staying, what they are looking at and what keywords they used to find you, among other things.

The website statistics tracking is an incredibly helpful tool to understand how people are using your site and determine how to improve it.

Where you host your website IS very important. Don't be tempted to cut corners here. If you try to save a few dollars, you will almost undoubtedly wind up frustrated and dealing with web server downtime, hard to use server management tools and less than knowledgeable Tech Support.

The Intermedia.net Tech Support is excellent; they usually respond in under an hour and can actually answer the most complicated questions you have. This has proven the case for me. No matter if it's dealing with Java scripts or database connection issues, logging problems or anything else. I have used them for five years, and they have only gotten better.

Action Step: To setup your website server, follow these steps:

1.) Go to Intermedia.net

2.) Click on Web Hosting.

3.) Sign-up for the *Basic Hosting* account. ($19.95/mo)

The *Basic Hosting* account is actually very robust, and can handle almost anything you want to do. This package includes online server management, your e-mail accounts, website statistics program, superb technical support, and plenty of bandwidth.

Also, you can use virtually any website design tool you're comfortable with, including Microsoft Expression Web, Adobe Dreamweaver, and Adobe Flash. You may also FTP your files up. I personally use Microsoft Expression Web, but any of these tools are excellent. In Chapter 4, I will go over the different web design tools.

Tip: After you register your domain name, here are the steps for how to point it to Intermedia.net, where your website is hosted, so that when you type your domain name in a web browser, e.g., www.yourname.com, your website will come up.

This example assumes you've registered your domain name through GoDaddy.com but it is almost the same process for any Domain Register.

1.) Login to your GoDaddy.com account.

2.) Click on My Account.

3.) Click Manage Domains.

4.) Click the domain name you'd like to modify.

5.) And finally click on the Name Servers, and enter this information ...

Name Server 1: NS2.INTERMEDIA.NET

Name Server 2: NS3.INTERMEDIA.NET

so it looks like this.

This will properly set up your domain name with your Domain Register. All Domain Registers work the same so no matter where you register your name, the process is the same for modifying your DNS server information to point to Intermedia.net DNS servers.

Definition: DNS stands for Domain Name Server. It features a pair of servers, one primary server and one for backup that stores the information on the server to send people to when they type in your web address.

Now, login to your Intermedia.net server Control Panel and click on DNS server and then on Domains. Enter your URL, leaving off the 'www.' portion so you will enter yourdomain. com, instead of www.yourdomain.com.

It will probably take three or four hours for the DNS server information to propagate throughout the Internet. Once that time has elapsed, when you go to a Web browser and enter your domain name, it will now show up with the default page that Intermedia.net puts up as a default before you've up-loaded any of your content to your website.

Congratulations! You're now ready to start building your website. But first ...

Forming an LLC or Inc.

The legal aspects of whether to form a LLC or Inc. are beyond the scope of this book. However, in general, an LLC is the preferred choice of a business entity. It is easy to form, easy to manage and, if formed as a single member LLC, it is treated as a pass-through entity so you can file the income on your personal taxes using Schedule C.

Forming an LLC to protect yourself is an essential step in starting your website. In most states, you can form an LLC online in about 30 minutes for around $100. The extra protection and added degree of credibility is easily worth the effort to prop-erly form an LLC for your business.

By forming an LLC, you benefit from the fact that you are now risking only the assets that are held in the business's name, instead of your being personally liable for any and all debts. It also looks more professional when people see you are an official business entity. Here is the BestWebsite, LLC graphic as an example:

BestWebsite™LLC.com
Simple Steps to Successful Websites

There are a number of procedural steps to follow to make sure your LLC is set up and run properly so it affords you the maximum protection. The most important are …

- Always display your company as a limited liability company by using the three letters, LLC. LLC should be prominently displayed on your website, on any payments made to you, and all payments should be payable to your business name; i.e., payable to Your Name, LLC.

- When signing contracts, always sign it appropriately; i.e., YourBusiness, LLC John Doe member.

- Keep a copy of your Articles of Organization supplied by your state at your place of business.

- Open a separate bank account in the business's name and keep all purchases and expenses separate from your personal account.

- File your Annual Report each year with your State.

(Please note: Each State is slightly different in how LLC's are governed; please check with your state to comply with local laws.)

To open a bank account in your business's name, you'll need an Employer Identification Number – also known as an EIN. After you have filed your LLC, you can call 1-800-829-4933. This is the government hotline to have your EIN number sent to you in the mail.

Your EIN number is just like a Social Security number, except it is meant to identify a business rather than a person. When you file your taxes, you will use your EIN number to identify your business.

Trademark Registration

Before I begin this section, I want to add some notes. Properly filing a Federal Trademark is no easy task. This is partly why Trademarks are so valuable. The United States Patent and Trademark Office (USPTO) knows it has no competitors. You cannot file a Trademark anywhere else, so they have no incentive to make it easy for you.

I also need to talk about First Use in Commerce. When you conduct your first transaction involving your product for money, you have, in effect, gained trademark rights to your name and may use the "TM" symbol. When you conduct your first transaction across state borders, you have gained national trademark rights.

It is this second example I'd like to expand upon. Before filing a Trademark, I recommend establishing basic national Trademark rights to your name by conducting at least one cross state border transaction. This is pretty easy to do on the Internet. The reason to do this is because it allows you to file directly for a Federal Trademark and not an Intent to Use application.

The Intent to Use application will require you to fill out another form and pay another fee after you have started using the Trademark in commerce. It's much easier just to file it once.

Why file with the federal USPTO? Is there a difference between having Trademark rights to a name and having federally registered Trademark rights? Yes, there are several important differences. When you establish your rights by using it in commerce only and not registering it officially with the USPTO, the burden of proof in a dispute lies with you to show that you have rights to the name.

Registering your business name with the USPTO as a Federal Trademark is a great idea for a number of reasons. It guarantees your exclusive right to use the mark in your business category. It creates additional credibility by using the ® symbol. And it increases the value of your business.

When people make payment to my business over the Internet, it shows they are making payment to …

BestWebsite® LLC

This looks professional and creates credibility, the two things I'm most interested in for my website. It shows that my company name is a registered Trademark, and that payment is going to an official business entity, a Limited Liability Company.

By registering your name, you are securing ownership of it for your particular industry. **If you build something successful, you will quickly discover people either use your name exactly or something**

confusingly similar. Either way, you are protected if you own the mark.

When you own the Trademark, it also increases the value of your business because you now have exclusive rights to that name and can brand it. It also gives you licensing rights for the name.

It takes about six months to get registered and costs $325. It is, however, money and time well spent. Many people use a lawyer to file for them, but that increases the cost of registration by $500 to $1,000. I can show you how to file it yourself, and learn about the process along the way.

Action Step: To see if anyone else has registered your name as a trademark or if confusingly similar names have been registered, follow these steps:

1. Go to www.uspto.gov.

2. Click on Trademarks (on the left hand side).

3. Click on Search Trademarks.

4. Click on Basic Search.

I'll use an example. When I was registering a trademark for BuySellCompany.com, I went first to the Basic Trademark search feature and typed in the name "BuySellCompany." Since I saw that this name was not registered, I entered the words individually, "Buy Sell Company," to see if any registrations came up.

There were only two other trademarks with those words in it. They were …

"MOVIE TRADING CO. BUY SELL MTC" and

"THE BUY FROM ME, SELL FOR FREE COMPANY"

Neither of these was confusingly similar to the mark "BuySell-Company" so I knew I had a good name to start. Even if there were another "buysellcompany" registered, I could still register the mark as long as I was in a different Goods and Services category. I would be careful to use the name in a definitively different business category.

You'll need to select the Goods and Services category that your business is in to file your Trademark. It is a good idea to determine this before you start the online application. It's a little difficult to locate on their website, so I've provided the link for you. Go to http://www.uspto.gov/main/trademarks.htm and click on Acceptable Identification of Goods and Services Manual.

Since BuySellCompany.com is a classified ad marketplace, I entered the search term "classified" and the following results were returned. (See table below.)

The third option was the most accurate description of my business so that is the one I used. You'll use this information when you're filling out the online application to file your trademark. Let's start that now.

Hit No.	Class	Description
1	016	Classified directories
2	033	Alcoholic beverages, namely, {indicate specific beverages} [cannot include beer since beer and related products such as ale, porter, stout, etc. are classified in Class 32]
3	035	Providing a website that enables users to post items for sale through on-line classified advertisements
4	035	Providing an on-line searchable database featuring classified ad listings and employment opportunities

Register the Name You Want...

Action step: To file your Trademark or to register the name you want, follow these steps:

1. Go to www.uspto.gov.

2. Click on Trademarks (on the left-hand side).

3. Click on File Online.

4. Click on Apply for a New Mark.

The application process looks like this:

Section 1: Applicant Information

Section 2: Mark Information

Section 3: Basis For Filing and Goods and/or Services Information

Section 4: Fee and Signature Information

Validation Page: Final review of information provided and form submittal

Remember, we are filing a Trademark for a name that has already been used at least once in a cross state border transaction.

You now have two choices, to file a:

Trademark/Servicemark Application – Principal Register or Trademark/Servicemark Application – Supplemental Register

The main difference is that, if you have made up your company name, such as Tazzy Tax, and you sell tax help guides, you are eligible to file on the Principal Register that affords you slightly more protection than the Supplemental Register. If you sell Baby Cribs and your business name is myBabyCribs, then you will file it on the Supplemental Register because the name is descriptive.

The difference between the Principal and Supplemental Register is that, if someone infringes on your Trademark and you are registered on the Principal, it is assumed that damages have occurred. If you are registered on the Supplemental, you will need to show what damages were incurred by the infringement.

Don't be too concerned at this stage about the difference between the two. To me, the point is to "have" a Federal Trademark. Yes, it's best to be on the Principal Register but it's certainly okay to have it listed only on the Supplemental. Plus, if you're still doing business in five years under the same name, you can have your Trademark also filed on the Principal, even if you started out on the Supplemental.

> **Tip:** If you are confused by which Register to file under, you can apply for the Principal Register; if your application is rejected, you can reapply to the Supplemental Register without losing your original filing date or having to pay an extra fee.

At this point in the application process, there are several things I'd like to mention. Since it costs $325 and takes six months to hear whether or not you filled out the form correctly, it does create a little pressure to fill out the form properly. So, here are my notes for the preliminary questions it asks you before you actually start the application process. I've included only notes on those things that I think might be confusing.

Notes for Preliminary Questions.

When the form asks, "what is your filing basis?" select "Use in Commerce Section 1A" since this means you are currently using the mark in commerce.

Notes for Section 1: Application Information

Since the form does not list Limited Liability Company as one of the choices for ownership of the mark, you'll need to select "other" and then select the entity type from the drop-down menu. I recommend you hold the trademark in your company's name and not in your personal name.

Notes for Section 2:

I recommend using standard characters to represent your mark as opposed to a stylized drawing. You have a better chance of getting it through using standard characters.

Notes for Section 3:

You'll need to provide a JPEG or PDF image of the mark you are intending to file to be used in commerce under the goods and services category you have selected. This could be a screenshot of your web page, where it shows how you are selling the goods or services that are related to the mark.

You'll also need to list the goods and services category you determined before you started the application. Each goods and services category is an additional $325.

The rest of the sections of the form are self-explanatory.

Well, congratulations, you can now put that aside and work on other aspects of your business. It will be six months before you hear something back from the government. For my part, filling out the applications myself allowed me to understand the application process more completely and appreciate the hard work they do at the Trademark office. With all the procedures that have to be followed and the research that they do for you to ensure correct ownership and assignment of Trademarks, it is impressive and is partly what makes a Trademark valuable to own.

If something is wrong, you'll most likely receive what is called an Office Action that details what additional information they need to file your mark. Once everything has been taken care of and it has been approved, you'll be mailed an official Trademark ownership certificate. Congratulations! You are the proud owner of a United States Federal Trademark!

800 Number, Business Cards and other things ...

The additional credibility that an 800-number provides your company, and the ease with which it can be set up definitely means you should have one. You can have the 800-number ring to any phone you choose and have a separate voice mail for incoming business calls to the 800-number. For instance, if you have the 800-number ring to your cell phone and some-one calls the 800-number, it will ring to your cell, but the voice greeting will be for your business. Then, to retrieve the voice-mail, you can either call in to hear it or have them automatically e-mail it to you in a .wav file.

Most online businesses do not generate a lot of 800-number phone calls and your monthly bill for the number will likely be $15-$30, a great bargain. There are a number of effective ways to differentiate yourself from your competitors and this is an excellent and easy way to do it.

The company I have been most pleased with is the company Kall8.com. It takes only a few minutes to get set up and you can receive calls immediately. They have the best online man-agement I've seen and are a fantastic bargain.

As far as business cards go, when you are just starting out, it's probably best not to order business cards. Too many things change in the beginning, such as your business name, colors, e-mail, phone number and tagline. Going to the office supply store and getting a packet of Avery business cards and design-ing them yourself allows you to print just 12 at a time.

I have a preference for the Avery Linen Finish or Glossy Finish. Here is an example of the business card that I designed:

BestWebsite™ LLC .com
Simple Steps to Profitable Websites

Nelson Bates, President
☎800.681.4176 ☎407.855.7112
✉best@bestwebsite.com

🌐 www.BestWebsite.com
- 13838 Fairway Island Dr. #1431 Orlando, FL 32837 -

* If you like the little phone, fax, e-mail and world icons, you can copy and paste them at BestWebsite.com/Bonus.

CH. 4 How to Design a Successful Website

- Web Design Software

- Graphics

Web Design Software

The point of this chapter is to describe the tools successful business owners use to run some of the Internet's most profitable websites. The sheer numbers of different tools and coding options are astounding and have only gotten more complicated. Luckily, with a clear understanding of what is available and how to use it, you can swiftly create and manage a great looking website that makes money.

When it comes to web design software and graphics software, a lot of Internet marketing books tend to gloss over the details or, at best, just list the different software tools you can use. I have my opinions on this, but it is interesting to note that two of the best selling Internet marketing books are written by multi-millionaires who did not do any design themselves, making them unable to provide useful advice to address the issues with which most people struggle to build a successful website.

It is important to note that, in general, most successful website business owners, do not build the entire websites themselves. They hire out some of the work, whether it is database design, graphics, special applications or Flash.

With that said, you will want to use the web design tool that provides you with the most features, is the easiest to use and has the ability for others to easily plug-in components like database coding, Java applets and Flash design, among others.

The vast majority of website owners, including myself, have chosen one of two tools to build and manage their websites. These are either Microsoft Expression Web (formally Microsoft FrontPage) or Adobe DreamWeaver (formally Macromedia DreamWeaver). There are many other tools, but these two are the most frequently used by successful website owners and are considered to be the most versatile and professional. Both of these tools are now far more similar than dissimilar.

Both tools allow you total control over almost every aspect of the design process, including importing graphics and Flash designs, database creation, creating forms, creating blogs, updating pages and backing up your site.

Some people cringe when talking about Microsoft Web Design products because those of you who used versions earlier than Microsoft FrontPage 2003 will remember that it was not a great design tool. The good news is that the latest release, Expression Web, is now an excellent design tool.

My preference is Microsoft Expression Web. One of the reasons is the amazing Database Wizard that is included with the software. You can create complex databases just by answering the questions the Wizard asks you about how you want your database to operate.

> **Note: See the end of this Chapter for specific database examples.**

Both web design tools allow you to have multiple people work on your website at one time, without the fear of deleting or writing over someone else's code. The goal here is to run a successful website but not necessarily to build it entirely yourself.

You'll probably want to hire out some of the aspects that you either can't do or are not good at doing and then have those components plugged into your website. This includes things like graphics, database coding and Flash design, among others. The end goal here is for you to become good at managing websites through one of these tools and not necessarily trying to build the websites entirely by yourself.

For instance, you might choose to have someone create the graphics for you and then someone else to build a template page. Learning these tools allows you to go in and add additional text and picture pages with ease. (I will show specific examples later in this chapter.)

You can use any design software you choose, however, using Expression Web or DreamWeaver gives you the best options for features, ease of use, and ability to have others work with you to grow your site in the future.

Structuring Website Templates

For many, building and managing a website is an incredibly difficult task; I have complete empathy with them because it is definitely a difficult thing to do. Most people never make it through the process of building a website that can actually earn money. Often, it is either incomplete, looks terrible or is abandoned out of frustration.

Since this is a key element in running a Successful Website, I'd like to give a specific example of how I built the "structure" of BestWebsite.com. I also call this the "template" for the site. By template, I mean designing the graphics and navigation structure that is common to all pages and, thus, will be seen on each page of the website.

You can see my logo graphic at the top left (created in Adobe Photoshop). I've chosen a top and bottom navigation structure so people can use the hyperlinks at the top and bottom of the pages to navigate through the site.

*This template is laid out using a Table.

You can build pages in either Expression Web or Dream-Weaver without having a web server set up to host your site. The software program saves the pages you create on your local hard drive. However, I recommend setting up your web server first and then logging into the site "live" and building the pages right onto the server so it is viewable on the Internet as soon as you save the page.

After opening the Expression Web application and logging into my server, I clicked the File menu, then New, then Blank Page and then Table, Insert and Table again, and then chose to insert a Table with 4 rows and 1 column and set the width of the Table to 800 pixels. I also set the borders to zero so the outline of the Table would not be visible to people who viewed the page through a browser. It was visible only to me so I could lay out the page during design and position the other elements, like graphics.

Then, I right clicked the third row down and selected cell properties and changed the background to light blue. I then used the Cell Corners and Shading to automatically create the black beveled look at the top and the shadow at the bottom of the Table.

Then I dragged and dropped the BestWebsite graphic into the top left and added the text hyperlinks "Home | Literary Agents | About Us | Contact Us" to the top and bottom of the page, the copyright notice at the bottom and phone and email at the top right. Then, I clicked Save As and chose Dynamic Web Template (more on this in a moment.) After that, I right clicked inside the third row, which I had given a blue background earlier, and then selected Manage Editable Regions (I will explain this below), entered "Main Body," Clicked on Add and then closed the dialog box.

Yes, that sounds a little complicated, but congratulations are in order because you've just been through one of the most difficult things to do when building your website, which is to build the general design for your website from which all other pages can be created. (I go into more detail about the advantages of creating a template for your site in a later chapter.)

Dynamic Web Template

So what is a Dynamic Web Template? It is an easy way to maintain a consistent look and feel throughout your website and this makes updates and adding pages a breeze. In the figure below, you will see a gray box. When you create a new page from this Dynamic Web Template, the <u>only</u> thing that can be changed on this new page is the content <u>inside</u> the shaded box. This is helpful because you, or anyone else you have log in to help you build your website, will never accidentally change the template of the website.

If you would like to change the template at any time; e.g., anything <u>outside</u> the shaded box, you just open the template page and make your change to it and it automatically updates every page in your website. It's a fantastic way to easily manage a website.

When you are ready to create a new page for your site, after you have created a template, just click File, New Page and then Attach Dynamic Web Template. You'll be looking at a page just like the one above, but you'll be ready to add your content and/or any pictures. Here's what I added to create my home page …

The picture was added as clip art from iStockPhoto.com for less than $20. It is a fantastic place to find excellent quality photos that are royalty free. You'll notice that the background is now green instead of the blue from the template. That is only because the picture's background was green. The rest of the pages of my site, like the Contact Us, About Us and other pages, all have the blue background.

Key Point About Those Who Make the Most Money Online

One of the key points about those who make the most money online is that they understand the basics of Web design… How to create a page, add and modify layout tables, insert graphics, add content, make modifications to it, and back it up.

This can all be taught in about 75 pages of reading. Unfortunately, the book that contains the 75 pages is 720 pages in length. Most people take one look at the book and say "No thank you."

It can be a confusing book if you don't know how to use it. The book I'm talking about is titled *Using Microsoft Expression Web* by Jim Cheshire; Published in 2007 by QUE.

It's not a book you read straight through. It's more of a reference book, and the good news is, most of it you don't need.

So what I've listed below is what you actually need from the book. If you take the information contained within the *Best Website* book you are reading now. And you use it with the knowledge you gain from the Chapters below. You have just set yourself ahead of almost every other person trying to make money online.

> Here are the Chapters and page numbers from the book *Using Microsoft Expression Web* - Published by QUE. (2007)
>
> **Chapter 7,** page 104-120 (Creating Pages and Content)
>
> **Chapter 8,** page 128, 140 (Using Web Page Views)
>
> **Chapter 9,** all of it (Using Tables and Layout Tables)
>
> **Chapter 14,** all of it (Using Graphics and Multimedia)
>
> **Chapter 21,** all of it (Using Dynamic Web Templates)

The Big Picture – Putting It All Together

It is incredibly easy to get bogged down in the details of building a website. There are so many different coding options, server architectures, database tools and other options – it can literally feel mind numbing. I recently watched the two minute introduction video for Expression Web on Microsoft.com and was truly amazed at how confused I felt about what they were talking about. They have a way of making it complicated sometimes.

Setting up your server with Intermedia.net gives almost limitless support for any type of server setup, software and database you'd like to use. And you can choose the least expensive web server hosting option and upgrade later if you need any additional add-ons, like an SQL database server or support for ColdFusion.

By using Expression Web or DreamWeaver, you have the maximum possible options for building your website. Both software programs offer free 30 day downloads and I encourage you to download them to see which one fits you better. They are now more similar than ever and if you know one of them, you can move to the other without being totally confused.

They retail for around $400 each so you might want to check eBay for used copies. Also, for most people, you can go with a slightly older version of Expression Web, which is FrontPage 2003 or Dreamweaver 7, which will make it much less expensive if budgeting is a concern.

Note: Many people get lost focusing on building their site and all these great features it's going to have and then think people will just come to their site and immediately recognize how great it is and buy or join. This is definitely not what happens; you must complete your site to the point of being launched and get to the marketing of the site. It will undoubtedly take longer than you think, require more money than you thought and be harder than expected.

When embarking on building a successful website, most people plan for a 100 mile journey, when, in reality, it is more like a 1,000 mile journey. This is why so many people never complete their site; they run out of time, money and patience.

The point here is to create a professional website as quickly as possible that looks good in any browser and on any display monitor and create it so it's easy to manage in the future, both by yourself and/or with anyone you hire to help.

There are so many different things you must do well to run a successful, profitable website; you can't get bogged down building your website. Just get the job done in excellent fashion and move on to the marketing and other duties as quickly as possible. Given the complexities of web design, this is not an easy task. I will go into more detail later about building your website.

Note: The reason I didn't mention Adobe Flash as a design tool is because the majority of websites don't need to be built using Flash. Plus websites are easier to manage in either Expression Web or Dreamweaver. I would only use Flash if building a visually intensive website such as those for movies and celebrities.

There is also the issue with Search Engine Optimization, which is definitely harder with a Flash designed site. It's okay to put Flash movies, banners or other elements into your website designed in one of the two tools I previously recommended, but don't use Flash to build your entire site.

Employing A Database – BuySellWebsite.com Example:

The database I built for BuySellWebsite.com was built in this manner. Just to give you an idea of how powerful this can be, I'll walk you through the steps of creating this database from scratch with no programming knowledge.

To start, I need to give a brief explanation of how BuySellWebsite. com operates. The website accepts classified listings and then displays them on its website for users to search. The pages are set up similarly to eBay's with a number of listings on each page where you can click the hyperlink to read more about each business for sale.

The database for BuySellWebsite.com ran most of this site. This is fantastic because it's like having an additional employee for free. After successful payment, the database took the listings, inserted them into the database, rotated the ads properly, deleted old listings, processed renewals, retrieved lost passwords and allowed users to update their listings.

Since the database basically ran the website, this is why having one is so valuable. Microsoft Expression Web will build the database structure almost entirely by answering questions about how you need the database to operate. Then Expression Web will write the database code in Active Server Pages (ASP) and insert it into your pages automatically. It is a brilliant tool if you know how to use it correctly. (Check the Bonus section for a Step by Step guide at BestWebsite.com/Bonus.)

Hire-Out Work Example: I want to give an example of how I use Microsoft Expression Web to manage my website and have others import work into it.

I needed a specific part of the database built that Microsoft Expression Web could not do through the Database Wizard. Specifically, I was trying to set up a tracking feature to track the number of times each classified ad was clicked on.

I contacted a database designer, and told him the specifics of what was needed as well as the username and password for logging into my web server. He then created the code on his computer, logged into my server through File Transfer Protocol (FTP), uploaded the code into the proper area and modified a few of the pages on the server that dealt with how the database operated.

This cost me about $200 and was well worth it because of the complicated nature of the coding as well as the value it added to my website. Many database designers use software that you have never heard of to create their code, and most of them prefer to log in via FTP to add it to your website. Both Expression Web and DreamWeaver allow database designers to connect to your web server in the manner they choose and add their code seamlessly into your website.

Graphics

Once again, I am describing how successful website owners build and run their websites, thus, the discussion about Graphics is based on this viewpoint. Most successful website owners can both maintain their website through one of the web design software tools previously mentioned and, at least, be able to modify their own graphics, if not create them using one of the two software tools listed below.

The reason why so many successful website owners can maintain their own website and modify their graphics is because this puts them in the driver's seat as far as being able to build the website they see in their minds' eye and create the marketing campaign around it.

I can't stress enough how important it is to know how to maintain your own website and modify your own graphics. Understanding these two things will automatically put you ahead of most of your competition and if you can bring yourself to the point of being able to build your own pages and design your own graphics, you can almost guarantee your site will have at least some success.

If you were to remove the graphics from almost any website, there almost would not be a website. Great quality professional graphics will definitely create credibility and make you stand out from the rest. There are really only two options with graphics – create your own or hire out the creation.

If you are creating your own, the two main types of software that website owners choose are Adobe Photoshop and Adobe Fireworks. These two can do great things for creating excellent graphics for your website and are especially designed to create website graphics.

I recommend these two not only because of their ability to build amazing graphics, but also because they will be in an original file format that can be modified by most other graphic designers if you need help. You would also have the ability to sell them along with your website to make additional money. (More on this in a later chapter.)

Photoshop is the more expensive, about $600, and Fireworks is $299. If you're upgrading from a previous version, they are about half that cost.

If you will be hiring out the creation of your graphics, a great way to get it done cost effectively is by going to eLance.com and posting a free ad for what you need and you will quickly have 20–30 people bidding on creating your graphics. Then, you just choose the one you are most comfortable with.

It pays to have some layout design already sketched out on paper as to what you want done as far as graphics are concerned. I'll give a couple of examples because sometimes people don't know where to start.

Probably the most important graphic on your site will be your main header graphic that contains your business name and slogan. As an example, the BestWebsite header graphic is simple text with a dividing line between the name and slogan.

BestWebsite™ LLC .com
Simple Steps to Successful Websites

This graphic is only 250 pixels by 50 pixels and is placed on the top of the page in a table with rounded borders to frame the graphic. This is the simplest of graphics created in Photoshop that uses a few effects like Bevel/Emboss and Drop Shadow.

If you hired someone to create this graphic for you on eLance.com, it would probably cost $50–$100. Another more complicated graphic is the one I did for BuySellWebsite.com that runs the entire length of the top of the website. It is 800 pixels wide by 70 pixels high.

(shown here smaller than actual size)

This graphic has the business name, slogan, background, and silhouette of people shaking hands. This graphic would probably cost between $150–$200 on eLance.com. How big your graphic is depends on how you intend to lay out your website.

I want to describe the difference between creating your own graphics and being able to modify graphics. If you are able to modify graphics, this means that you are able to open an existing graphic in a graphic design tool and be able to do some general modifications to it. As an example, I got this billboard sign from clipart, opened it in Photo-  shop and added the words "Advertise Here" in red and 1.800. CALL.NOW in black.

Being able to modify graphics also entails resizing images and cropping them. If you try to resize a graphic in either Dreamweaver or Expression Web, the graphic loses resolution and looks pixilated. This is why it's good to be able to know how to modify graphics because you can open the graphic in your graphic design tool, and properly resize the image without losing any image quality.

Conversely, if you have to rely on a graphic designer to make minor changes, you will quickly deplete your budget and add significant time to the design process.

Being able to create graphics is just as it sounds, it is the ability to start with a blank screen and create images from nothing.

> **Most successful website owners don't know how to create graphics from scratch. However, they do know how to modify existing graphics.**

Key To Making Money Online

Key: I'd like to describe one of the key differences between those who make money online, and those who lose money online. Those who make money online know about the 100% rule, which is that they don't need things to be 100% correct before they move on. I'll give an example:

When a friend was designing a website in the past, he needed a login function to check for a user ID and password to be able to view a membership section of the website. There wasn't any sensitive information located in the membership section, so security was not high priority. Instead of hiring out the database design he needed to be able to validate logins, he just used a submission form where people entered their username and password, and it took them directly to the members' section without checking to see if the entered information was correct.

Since he knew that the vast majority of people, probably 99% or more, would fill out the new user form first and then attempt to login, he knew it was fine not to have it 100% correct.

There were several reasons to do this. The most important is that he still had control over his website because he could easily create a login function himself using the tools provided by the Web design software. He also saved money that he would have needed to spend on the designer.

Having as much control as possible over your own website is essential. Also, saving time and money is critically important. Most of the time this advice is met with aversion, and I can understand the criticism. However**, I am merely stating one of the differences between people who make money online and people who don't. Those who do, know how to build the function they need quickly without involving an outside designer or spending a lot of money.**

I have seen many websites never get off the ground, mostly because they were trying too hard to make things 100% right at the beginning. Think about the aspects of your website that can be solved the easy way first. Then, once your website is up and running and you understand how people use your website, you can come back to that aspect and correct it or possibly realize that nothing more needs to be done.

My intention with this book is not to describe the Utopian way to build a website; it is to describe how successful business owners build and run their websites to earn significant money online.

CH. 5 Remarkable Internet Marketing

At the beginning of this book, I listed the BestWebsite Essential 9™ and the first thing on that list was to Create a Remarkable Website. In the long run, it is far less expensive to build a remarkable website than it is to advertise an average one. Give people a **reason** to talk about your website and they will do your promotion for you!!

Come up with a remarkable aspect for your product, service, business, etc. and then incorporate it into your website.

Let me define what remarkable is. Remarkable is anything you do that someone else talks about or remarks about. So, by definition, it is remarkable.

Let me give an example. When we released a Press Release for the BestWebsite Essential 9, it took only one day before Yahoo! News had picked it up and distributed it through their news network. So, by definition, the BestWebsite Essential 9 is remarkable because Yahoo! News chose to talk about.

This concept is clearly described in Seth Godin's marketing books like **Purple Cow**, **FREE Prize Inside** and **The Dip**. I haven't seen anyone be truly a step ahead in the marketing game like he is. He is definitely worth reading.

Understanding the process of creating a remarkable website is very helpful. Let me give another example ...

My last business was BuySellWebsite.com. It was remarkable because it was the #1 most visited website for sale marketplace. Many people remarked about it in e-mails, blogs and news stories, essentially doing my promotion for me!

Of course, I didn't start out number one. If I remember right, I started out with 17 competing businesses ranked ahead of me. However, after employing the marketing techniques I'm showing in this book, I was able to achieve the number one ranking.

The reason why having at least one remarkable aspect to your business is so important, is because the effectiveness of the marketing techniques talked about in the next two chapters will be multiplied many times over.

For example, if you first achieve some reasonable search engine rankings and begin to get traffic to your website, and **IF** you have a remarkable aspect to your website, the people that visit your website will talk about you to their friends, on their blogs, and in e-mails or possibly link to you from their website.

This is incredibly helpful and makes everything you do easier. The more links you have pointing to you, the easier it is to get higher search engine rankings and far better keywords. You will also enjoy the traffic that they send you as well as additional credibility offered by their recommendation.

> **If someone else recommends you, it is far easier to make a sale than if that visitor comes to you through a paid advertisement.**

As I work on the promotion for this book, my job is to find a remarkable aspect to promote it. It's going something like this ...

There are many Internet marketing books out there. I'm trying to write one that is short, cuts out the clutter and shows a clear path to success. That in-of-itself is remarkable.

But I'd like an additional remarkable aspect. The idea I'm leaning towards is giving away a free optimized link from Best-Website.com to your website with every book sold. I believe that is remarkable because, just by purchasing the book, you can help your search engine rankings ... **and no other book can do that!**

For me, this is the perfect gift to give away; Seth Godin refers to it as the FREE Prize. Everyone should have one for his or her website. It's something that costs you a little, but has high perceived value, and something no one else is doing.

In this case, the cost is minimal. I just need to spend the time doing the programming to make it automated. The perceived value and actual value are high. And I know of no one else doing this.

There are literally hundreds of ideas like this that you can come up with to offer alongside whatever it is you're selling. Spending time to come up with one is well worth the effort.

CH. 6 Search Engine Optimization Strategies

When Search Engine Optimization is done correctly, you can enjoy a steady stream of interested visitors to your website ready to buy your products. If done incorrectly, you will unfortunately be among the other 98% of Internet entrepreneurs losing money online.

I have seen many examples of great looking websites that lost lots of money because there was no traffic. Understanding where to spend your money and what to spend your time on is essential to success in Internet marketing.

I'd like to break Search Engine Optimization into two parts: **The Basics** and **Second Stage SEO**. Neither category is necessarily difficult to implement. However, if not done correctly or not at all, the strategies are useless. The true power comes when you do both of them because they multiply each other's effectiveness.

The Basics essentially refers to keyword research, and the changes you make to your website to optimize it for the search engines. **Second Stage SEO** is how to get high-quality websites to link to you.

Even though I refer to it as the Basics, it is not basic knowledge. Information about how to implement the basic strategies I outline here is difficult to find, sometimes confusing and often contradictory.

Now I'd like to describe some of the basic Internet marketing techniques that successful website owners, myself included, use to promote their websites.

The Basics can be summarized in two steps for optimizing your website for search engines:

I.) Select the keywords that you are going to target.

2.) Make the changes necessary on your website to optimize those keywords for the search engines.

The Basics: Keyword Selection Process

Selecting the proper keywords sometimes is more difficult than it might appear. The way you go about it depends on if you are starting your website from scratch or if you are optimizing an existing website. It also depends on how competitive the keywords are you're trying to reach.

What I am about to describe is a very effective and easy way to come up with a keyword list to target that gets results very quickly. I define "getting results" by obtaining first page rankings on the major search engines for a particular keyword.

Let me sum up the process first and then go into specifics. Many times, when you are starting out, you don't have a handle on how you'd like to represent your website, its products and the angle from which you want to sell, which is okay. As you move through the startup process, it becomes clear and you can change your target keywords accordingly.

But it's good to get some keywords going right from the start and put them on the first few pages of your site to let the search engines start recognizing your site, what your site is about and establish your website's existence since the longer your site is up, the better it will rank.

As an example of how I started the keyword process to sell the book you are reading now, I came up with some general keywords I thought people who would be interested in purchasing my book might search for. I then selected several highly targeted keywords within the general list and targeted those first because (1) they are easy to get in a short amount of time (generally less than a month) and (2) they convert into sales at a very high rate because they are so targeted.

One of the general keywords I started with for this book was the keywords: "Internet marketing." I really like the free keyword tool by WordTracker.com (http://freekeywords. wordtracker.com) because their tool shows an estimated number of searches performed for that keyword compiled from MetaCrawler.com and DogPile.com, which are search engines that search the search engines. That sounds weird, I know, but try it for a search once and you'll see it's pretty good!

These two search engines are unique in that they actually release their raw search data, meaning it shows you how many times a particular keyword was searched for the day before. Google, Yahoo, MSN and all other major search engines are very secretive about their search data and don't release it to anyone.

Some people might say it can be inaccurate to use limited search data. However there is no 100% accurate tool available anywhere. Plus, when you use it in conjunction with Google Suggest (which I will explain in a moment), it is great because you are essentially querying their database of search terms, so you're getting the data right from the source! And it also acts as a backup to the results provided by WordTracker.

So, back to WordTracker's Free Keyword Tool, I type in "Internet marketing" and this list comes up.

Searches	Keyword
9,424	total searches
1705	internet marketing
442	internet marketing services
419	internet marketing strategy
354	internet marketing service
328	internet marketing strategies
262	hotel internet marketing
246	internet marketing online
211	dallas internet marketing
186	dallas internet marketing services
179	dallas internet marketing consultant
40	internet marketing book
14	internet marketing books

What I'm looking for is a laser targeted keyword for my product and the two that jump out are "Internet marketing book" and "Internet marketing books." To show you how I came to that conclusion, I'll walk you through the decision process.

I've included the top ten results in the above list and I omitted a number of results to show "Internet marketing book" and "Internet marketing books," which were further down the list. This list showed me the keyword "Internet marketing book" was searched for an estimated 40 times yesterday on all search engines combined. They use a formula to calculate the estimated daily search volume that includes Google, Yahoo, MSN and others.

This is a low searched for keyword, however, it is laser targeted. Since I also know that the search engines often include the plural as a single result, meaning "Internet marketing book" and "Internet marketing books" with an "s" are viewed as the same thing, it means that there is a combined total search volume of 54 per day across all search engines and I only need to target one of the keywords to cover both.

A great complement to WordTrackers Keyword Tool is Google Suggest (http://www.google.com/webhp?complete=1&hl=en); you can also go to Google.com and type in "suggest" for the link. If you type in "Internet marketing," it starts suggesting keywords for you in real time. This list is extraordinarily helpful because it shows the ten most relevant keywords that have the keywords you typed contained within them. Google's Suggest list for the keyword "Internet marketing" looks like this ...

Keyword	Number of Results in Millions
internet marketing	398
internet marketing online	232
internet marketing affiliate program	5
internet marketing company	186
internet marketing services	280
internet marketing center	195
internet marketing strategies	116

internet marketing book	61
internet marketing solution	172
internet marketing blog	174

The number of results, which is Google's number showing how many pages on the internet contain the keyword is a reasonable indicator of how competitive a keyword is. However, it is only a guide because of how they calculate the number of results. For instance, they count a page as a 'result' that contains the keyword "Internet" and "marketing" on the same page. However, that is not really a competitor of yours.

In this list, the keyword "Internet marketing book" is the most relevant and specific for what I'm selling and is also less competitive than the others based on the number of results.

If I can obtain a first page ranking for this keyword on each search engine, I can reasonably expect to capture a 20% click through rate, which means I can expect approximately eleven visitors per day from this one keyword. Note that with keywords that are this targeted, they convert at an incredibly high rate and 10% to 20% is very common. This means that I will likely be selling one to two books per day from this one keyword alone.

From the time I selected the keyword "Internet marketing book" until the time I had a first page ranking on Google was only 11 days. This is quite incredible for all the people out there who have started an Internet business and have spent months and months getting zero sales. It is very helpful for your motivation and your psyche to be making money almost from the start and, hence, why I recommend using laser targeted keywords to boost traffic.

Since laser targeted keywords are much easier to get, I didn't have to do a lot to achieve the ranking. Here's what I did ...

I had the basic pages of my website up with basic design and text as well as my book for pre-sale, including a Home Page, About Us page, Contact Us page, and the first four chapters of the book split onto four different pages.

I then opened my Home Page using Microsoft Expression Web and right clicked the page, selected Page Properties and made the Title of the page *Internet Marketing Book* (labeled 1. below). I also added it to the meta keywords section (labeled 2. Below) that is under the same page's properties tab. Then, I selected OK.

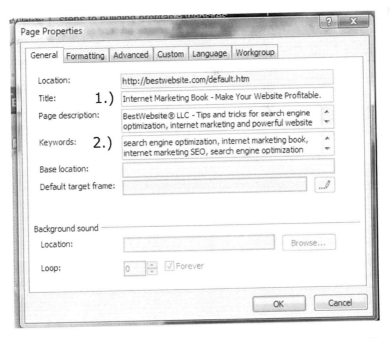

I then added the keyword "Internet marketing book" to the top of every page in small type. The closer to the top of the page, the more emphasis the search engines place on the keyword. (labeled 1. below)

This is a cinch to do if you designed your site using a Dynamic Web Template or other template-based system because you only need to update one page.

As far as the modifications to my website went, that was all I needed. By making the modifications to my website for this keyword, it was easy for the search engines to understand what my website was about.

The only thing I needed was a few other quality websites linking to mine to give the search engines enough of a reason to rank my website on the first page.

Since this is a low competition keyword, I only need a few other quality websites linking to me. We built a Squidoo.com webpage (Squidoo.com/BestWebsite) that contained the first four chapters of my book and pointed all the hyperlinks back to BestWebsite.com.

I then purchased a Yahoo Directory Listing for $299 a year and used the free service, Digg.com (talked about in the next chapter), to submit my chapters **and that was it! Eleven days later, Google had BestWebsite.com ranked on the first page!**

So, here it is, if you go to Google.com and type in "Internet marketing book," it returns the following results on the first page with the keyword "Internet Marketing Book" displayed as the title linking to BestWebsite.com (labeled 1. below)

> I'd like to give credit to my business partner, Amber Massey, who actually did the work to create the Squidoo pages. She has written a great tutorial to building your first Squidoo Page that is included in the next chapter.

For most Internet businesses, you'll likely be able to find three or four laser targeted keywords that you can start with. I've listed my first one here, "Internet marketing book," and I have also chosen three others from the general categories of "search engine optimization," "SEO" and "Internet marketing."

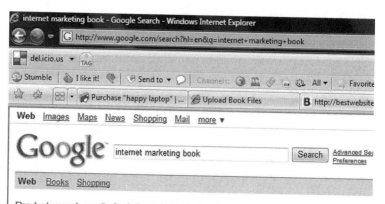

1.)

Starting out with this method allows me to get incredibly targeted traffic very quickly and start making sales almost immediately! It also does another thing, by targeting the keyword "Internet marketing book," it also indirectly targets the keyword Internet marketing. And the same goes for the other laser targeted keywords.

The reason why you don't want to target the big keywords first is because they take so much longer to get results and you have to do a lot more to get them. The keyword "search engine optimization" is one of the most fiercely competitive keywords on the Web. To give you an idea of how difficult it is to obtain a first page ranking for this particular keyword, consider this ...

If you go to Google and type in "search engine optimization," the websites listed on the first page, on average, have been on the Internet since 1998, and the average number of links pointing to each of them is more than 4,100.

Don't let me scare you, though. Most keywords are nowhere near this bad. The longer your website is up, with some optimization as well as knowing how to get quality websites to link to you, you can achieve excellent results as well.

The Basics: Keyword Selection Process II

In this particular keyword example, I'd like to use the example of one of my good friends, Sarah Martini, starting a photography website to sell her photography services (SarahMartini. com). This is a local service, which automatically makes it a niche market. She lives in the Los Angeles area; thus, the first keyword that comes to mind is "headshots." Here are the top

10 searches using WordTracker's Free Keyword tool that contain that keyword:

Searches	Keyword
1,989	total searches
419	headshot
326	boom headshot
171	headshots
54	actor headshots
52	paintball headshot
38	los angeles headshot photographers
33	female headshots
29	gears of war headshot
22	baby headshot
21	headshots nyc

The sixth one down is perfect, "Los Angeles headshot photographers." Since I'd like to get at least two to three more laser targeted keywords, I typed in "Los Angeles photographer." And the following list was returned: (following page)

Out of this list, we selected "Los Angeles Photographer" with 76 searches per day (you'll notice I added the plural form of the keyword to the search total) and "Los Angeles commercial photographers" with 17 searches and, finally, "LA headshot" with 7 searches per day that came from another search we did.

Searches	Keyword
461	total searches
47	los angeles fashion photographers
47	los angeles photographers
38	los angeles headshot photographers
35	fashion photographers in los angeles
29	los angeles photographer
22	model photographers in los angeles county
17	commercial model photographers in los angeles
17	los angeles commercial photographers
15	headshot photographers in los angeles
15	los angeles wedding photographers
14	head shot photographers in los angeles

So the list looks like this ...

Los Angeles headshot photographers (38 searches)

Los Angeles Photographer(76 searches)

Los Angeles commercial photographers (17 searches)

LA headshot (7 searches)

It's not just about getting the keyword with the maximum number of searches. It's also about targeting as specifically as possible. I love working with websites like this because such dramatic results can be achieved so quickly.

Since she doesn't have chapters of a book like I did to put on-line, she'll likely need to write three or four articles targeting each of these keywords. The articles don't need to be lengthy. They just need to be relevant and engaging and related to photography. Then, she used the same method I described above to target the "Internet marketing book" keyword.

Since this example is slightly more in depth, let's go over the steps in detail. At this point, she has her website up with the basic pages; these are a Homepage, About Me page, Prices page, and a Sample Gallery page. After she completed writing her three articles, she posted them on her website in the following manner…

1. Open her website using Microsoft Expression Web;

2. Then click New, Page, from the Dynamic Web template, which is the template file you created earlier;

3. Then paste your article onto the page and click File, Save As and save the file as www.sarahmartini.com/ Los-Angeles-headshot-photographers.htm

This file is saved in the root directory of her web server. The closer it is to the root directory, the more important search engines place on the page (although it's not a huge boost, everything helps.) It also makes it easy for them to recognize the keywords. You'll also want to use the keyword as the Title of the page and at least once more somewhere in the body of the article.

In the past, how to target keywords for the search engines properly used to be incredibly technical. But the search engines are very smart now. If you target each keyword this way and have other high-quality websites linking to you that are in your industry, you'll have no trouble achieving great rankings.

The more competitive a keyword is, the more websites you'll need linking to you to achieve a great ranking. This really can't be overemphasized. The main reason why one website ranks better than another is because of the number of high quality relevant links pointing to that website or webpage.

Yahoo and Google are very smart. They have focused on one of the keys to a successful high ranking website that is almost impossible to duplicate. And that's the fact that if someone has taken the time to create a link to your website and hundreds or thousands of people have done this, that means that hundreds or thousands of people have decided you have quality information and are worthy of a high-ranking.

Of course, spam artists have tried to get around this with link farms and questionable linking strategies. Yahoo, Google and MSN can easily spot these tactics and nullify them. There is no reason to try to trick the search engines. Instead of having them working against you, you'll set it up so the search engines work for you! I will discuss link building in-depth in the next chapter.

Let's clear a few things up. I'm sure there are questions like: how do you know how competitive a keyword is? How do you know if the keyword receives enough searches? How long will it take to achieve first page rankings? What percent will convert into sales?

There are no absolute answers to any of these questions because of the number of variables involved. It depends on the product you're selling, how hard you work on your Internet marketing, how good your website is, and how tough the keywords are you're going after.

I like to think of it like this – immediately go after the laser targeted keywords because if you're not able to get those, there's no way you can get the bigger ones. And the good news about going after the laser targeted keywords is that you can get feedback much sooner and adjust your strategy accordingly.

I'll give a few specific examples of keywords and the number of searches they receive. For instance, "search engine optimization" receives more than 24,000 searches per day. This is a huge keyword and a first page ranking will likely mean thousands of visitors per day to your website.

If you're selling a low profit item, you might need this much traffic to turn a good profit. On the other hand, if you have a keyword like "Los Angeles headshot photographer," which receives only 38 searches per day, that might be all you need since each photography package sold could earn thousands of dollars.

There are two main keyword tools that can help you in selecting keywords. One of these I've already mentioned which is WordTracker.com. Up until now I've only spoken of the free keyword tool. They also have a paid membership service that essentially ranks the keywords for you as well as how competitive they are.

The paid membership tool can be very helpful, but there is also a lot of data there and it can be confusing, especially if you're just starting out. You might feel you have to start out with the perfect keyword. I've seen this many times where people get analysis paralysis and will not move forward because they're presented with too much data.

You can save a lot of time in the beginning by just using the free WordTracker keyword tool and using Google Suggest to get an idea of other related keywords you might not have found through WordTracker's tool. Then, if need be, come back in a month or two after you've seen how your laser targeted keywords are doing and purchase a WordTracker membership to find additional keywords.

The other main paid keyword tool is KeywordDiscovery. com. I don't have as much experience with them as I do with WordTracker. However, I have heard good things about them.

Over the many years I have been doing this, it is my opinion that the free keyword tool, combined with using Google Suggest, is all most people will need. I have also learned that almost any keyword service you use, whether paid or free, will return similar results so don't feel like you have to use any one in particular.

One of the most difficult aspects of building a profitable website is trying to get past all the clutter. There's so much confusion and so many things to do that compete for your time, don't get hung up and spend all your time on something that's unimportant.

Pay-Per-Click

There is something I haven't talked about yet, and that is pay-per-click advertising. Both Yahoo and Google offer this service where you bid how much you're willing to pay for each click. I liked pay-per-click three to four years ago when you bid a certain amount; based on that bid, if you were in the third-place, your ad would show up in the third ranking whenever someone completed a search for that keyword.

At this point, however, for virtually every keyword pay-per-click is extremely competitive and it is almost impossible to turn a profit. I actually still recommend doing it, but keep it within a limited scope. Their tools are so complex that you can spend many, many hours trying to optimize your pay-per-click campaign.

For instance, using Google AdWords (adwords.google.com), from the time you open the account to the time your ads are live, can be less than hour. They have an amazingly fast and easy tool that gets you started but that is part of the problem. It's too easy and too fast and everyone does it.

Then, the complexity begins when you attempt to optimize your campaign. They make you feel like you will eventually figure out the combination that makes it profitable, but the vast majority of people do not. The competition is fierce and, as I said, it is almost impossible to turn a profit.

I do still recommend it because you can get quality traffic based on keywords you select and track the sales to determine which keywords produce the most sales. This is incredibly valuable knowledge to have. Although this is not verified, I do believe that Google uses this information also to rank your website organically. Because they know if you're paying for a particular keyword, it is likely relevant to your website.

In my opinion, part of the reason that the two Google founders are both ranked in the top ten richest billionaires in the world is because the AdWords tool they developed is a brilliant device that extracts money from you and gives it to them. I'm being a little harsh on them, but it is essentially true.

CH. 7 Second Stage SEO

Second stage search optimization (SEO) occurs after you have your basic website at least up and running and you've made the necessary changes to your website to optimize it for the search engines. You are now ready for second stage SEO, which has a lot to do with building quality links to your website.

A link from a quality website is from a website that search engines already rank high for a competitive keyword in your industry. Another way to measure it is to use Alexa. com. If the website ranks within the top 1,000, it is a very high-quality link; if it ranks within the top 25,000, it is still a high-quality link.

Note: Alexa.com's ranking system becomes inaccurate beyond the top 25,000. Also, a website can still be considered a high-quality link even if it doesn't rank within the top 25,000. As long as the website ranks well for a good keyword in your market, a link from that website to yours counts as a high-quality link.

I'd like to mention briefly one of the biggest misconceptions of ranking high in the search engines. Many people believe that it is the keyword optimization done to your website that has the largest impact on your rankings.

In the past, this was true. However, with today's very smart search engines, the most important factor is other quality websites linking to yours.

As an example, I want websites linking to me that have to do with Internet marketing, search engine optimization, website design and building profitable websites in general.

It is incredibly difficult to get quality websites within your market to link to you. However, since you have this book, I can show you an easy way to obtain high-quality links pointing to your website that come from pages that have the right keywords in them, that the search engines place high value on and, most importantly, that you have control over!

I don't, however, want to lessen the importance of creating a remarkable website in the first place. By having a remarkable aspect to your website and then employing the Second Stage SEO I go into in this chapter, you can quite literally create amazing traffic flow to your website.

It's easy to see which websites search engines believe are important by typing in a keyword for your industry and seeing who is ranked on the first few pages.

The following list shows seven high quality links that you can get that point back to your website and most are free. Do not underestimate the power of these links; each of these is a heavy hitter in its own right. And, when set up properly, they can produce remarkable traffic and dramatically boost your search engine rankings for your website.

1. Squidoo.com

2. Digg.com

3. Del.icio.us

4. StumbleUpon.com

5. Yahoo Directory Listing

6. PRWeb.com

7. Majon.com

Free Squidoo Page

Building a free Squidoo.com page (they refer to them as Lenses) is a fantastic way to not only boost search engine rankings for your own website by linking back  to it, but also to gain valuable traffic from the business oriented Squidoo community. Keep in mind that creating unique, useful, remarkable content is actually the best way to get your Squidoo page (and therein, whatever site it is promoting) to perform well in search engines.

Be mindful not to just recycle carbon-copies of your existing content onto a Squidoo page as this won't be much of a win. Use your Squidoo page to make a new statement about your website topic and your efforts will be rewarded.

Alexa.com ranks Squidoo within the top 1,000 most visited sites on the Internet (currently #673.) This is part of the reason why it is such an important link to your website.

There are a couple of ways to use Squidoo.com. If you're not yet ready to build a full website, you can start by building a Lens here to get things going and to see others' comments about your work, which can be very helpful. Then, at a later time, when you're ready to build your website, you can create links pointing back to it.

However, if you already have your website up and running and you have written your three or four articles and chosen your laser targeted keywords, then you're ready to go! Check out Amber Massey's advice on **Creating Your First Squidoo Lens** at the end of this chapter.

You're welcome to see our Lens at Squidoo.com/BestWebsite as an example.

Read more in depth about Squidoo.com at the end of this chapter.

Digg News, Del.icio.us Bookmarks and StumbleUpon

digg™ del.icio.us® StumbleUpon®

These three websites are an excellent way not only to boost search engine rankings, but also possibly to generate tens of thousands of unique visitors to your website from these on-line communities.

I'll give a brief description of each and then go into how to use them to help you.

According to Wikipedia, Digg.com is a community-based popularity website with an emphasis on technology and science articles but recently expanding to a broader range of categories, such as politics and entertainment. It combines social bookmarking, blogging, and syndication with a form of non-hierarchical, democratic editorial control.

News stories and websites are submitted by users, and then promoted to the front page through a user-based ranking system. This differs from the hierarchical editorial system that many other news sites employ. However, the news stories are not independently verified and, as such, they can only be viewed as user generated content.

Wikipedia, defines Del.icio.us as.

The website del.icio.us (pronounced as "delicious") is a Social Bookmarking web service for storing, sharing, and discovering web bookmarks. The site was founded by Joshua Schachter in late 2003, and was acquired by Yahoo! in 2005.

And finally, Wikipedia describes StumbleUpon.com as ... a web browser plugin that allows its users to discover and rate webpages, photos, videos, and news articles. These webpages are typically presented when the user – known within the community as a Stumbler – clicks the "Stumble!" button on the browser's toolbar.

StumbleUpon chooses which new webpage to display based on the user's ratings of previous pages, ratings by his/her friends, and by the ratings of users with similar interests; i.e., it is a recommendation system, which uses peer and Social Networking principles. There is also one-click blogging built in as well. Users can rate, or choose not to rate, any webpage with a thumbs up or thumbs down, and clicking the Stumble button resembles "channel-surfing" the Web. Toolbar versions exist for Firefox, Mozilla Application Suite and Internet Explorer, but it also works with some independent Mozilla-based browsers.

eBay acquired StumbleUpon in May 2007 for $75,000,000.

Ok, so how do you use them to help you!...

A brief look at how the search engines recognize links is helpful. For instance, Google has an algorithm in their search engine called "QDF" which stands for Query Deserves Freshness.

In practical terms this means that a news story submitted to Digg.com can literally show up in Google's search engine database results within minutes. If you submit an article to Digg.com, it will likely be indexed by the search engine and appear within the search results within the hour.

They've added this to their algorithm to make sure breaking news stories are always well represented immediately within the search engine. This also makes it an excellent search engine optimization tool for you because it's so fast.

The best way to use Digg.com is to submit a high-quality article that has the keywords you're targeting within the title and/or the description.

> By the way, Digg.com users love articles like this. Things that are lists and quick easy reads tend to be dug a lot and frequently reach the Digg home page.

As an example: When I posted the first four chapters of this book on my website, I had saved them as four separate files. The first chapter was the first article I submitted. Chapter I contained the BestWebsite Essential 9 located here ...

http://BestWebsite.com/The-Essential-9.htm

The best way to Digg it is to open the page you'd like Dug on your website using your web design software. And then copy and paste the following code at the bottom of the article. (You can copy this code from their site at digg.com/tools/.)

```
<script src="http://digg.com/tools/diggthis.js"
type="text/javascript"></script>
```

Then, when you click File and Save and view your page through a browser, a new button will appear at the bottom of your page that looks like this ...

Now, simply click the *digg it* button and if you don't already have a digg.com account, it will ask you to set one up, which only takes a moment. After that, it will ask you for title for the article; in this case, I chose…

The 9 Most Important Profitable Website Tips.

It will then ask you for a short description for the article, which I wrote as…

"The BestWebsite® Essential 9 - is the nine most important things you can do to make your website a remarkable success."

Then, choose the most appropriate category, i.e., business, entertainment, tech, etc., and click submit and within a few minutes, you'll see your story appear in the Upcoming Articles section.

You can see what's being listed right now for the category of business at … http://digg.com/news/world_business/upcoming

Both Yahoo and Google will likely index the article within the hour, and you'll have an excellent high-value link pointing to your website that has the right keywords contained within it.

If your article is well written and the information is remarkable, you have a chance of making the Digg.com Front Page. This alone can send tens of thousands of visitors to your website in a single day.

> Please see the free bonus section at BestWebsite.com/ Bonus for articles on how to do this as this method changes frequently.

Now on to del.icio.us and bookmarking with them. While Digg is centered on a public forum, del.icio.us is centered on a personal forum. What that means is, when you bookmark a webpage using del.icio.us, it saves it to your own personal page. You can see mine at http://del.icio.us/bestwebsite, my own personal page of saved links to other web pages.

The reason it is a great search engine optimization tool is because you can choose a page to bookmark, which creates a link to the page, then you can also choose a title, description and tag words (tags are essentially keywords).

For instance, when I bookmarked the page for the BestWeb-site Essential 9, it looked like this ...

The 9 Most Important Profitable Website Tips. save this

The BestWebsite Essential 9tm - The nine most important things you can do to make your website a remarkable success. 1.) Create a Remarkable Website.. It is far cheaper to build a remarkable website than it is to advertise an average one. Come up with.. to Internet marketing book search engine optimization strategy tips services ... saved by 12 other people... on Oct 14

This is fantastic because the search engines index which pages are being linked to from del.icio.us. The more bookmarks the better and, if you've already bookmarked the page, when other people bookmark the page, it suggests the tags (keywords) you've already chosen to associate with the URL.

You can bookmark as many pages as you'd like and choose as many tags as you'd like. It literally takes only a few minutes to bookmark your first page.

There are several ways to bookmark your pages; the way I chose was to paste the following onto the bottom of each page of my website that I'd like to bookmark.

■ Save This Page

In my case it was at the bottom of each chapter page, but for you it will likely be at the end of each article page. The hyperlink points to http://del.icio.us/post, then just click on the hyperlink and, if you don't already have an account, it will ask you to sign up, which only takes a second.

After you've signed up, it will automatically fill in the URL of the page you're bookmarking and you choose a title, description and tags (keywords). Then, click save and that's it! It's now live on the page. You can edit it at any time or delete it entirely.

> You don't have to paste the code on your website or web pages to save it to del.icio.us. You can just create an account with them and click "post" and copy and paste the URL you'd like to bookmark. Then, go through the same process of choosing title, description and tags.

Go ahead and bookmark all of your articles and tag them accordingly. Now everyone on del.icio.us is able to see what you bookmarked and, if they find it useful, they can bookmark it as well under their del.icio.us page.

If enough people bookmark your page in a short amount of time, it can reach their Hot List or Popular List, both of which can drive tens of thousands of visitors to your website. Also, many times when an article reaches the hot list or popular list on del.icio.us, it will also make the front page on Digg.com

> Please see the free bonus section at BestWebsite.com/Bonus for articles on how to do this as it changes frequently.

StumbleUpon.com is a great user-based community, where you can submit your articles and your website for other users to "stumble upon." Users install a toolbar that runs at the top of their browser, where they can submit websites and web pages that they like that are recommended to other users when they click the stumble button or when they search for it through the StumbleUpon.com website.

It's very easy to get started. Just install the toolbar from the Stumble Upon homepage, which only takes a few minutes. Then, browse to the page you'd like to submit and click on the "I like it" button and the URL and title will already be filled in for you. Just type in a brief review of the page and select the tags (keywords) for the page and click submit. And that's it!

Your pages are now submitted into the Stumble Upon engine and other users can find your articles and website by stumbling upon it. You almost need to see it in action to fully appreciate how to works.

All three of these Social Networking sites can do wonders for building link popularity, better search engine rankings and large amounts of additional traffic if your pages become popular. I'm sure you can start to see why creating remarkable content is so helpful because of how quickly traffic can snowball if your content is useful and people Digg it, Bookmark it and StumbleUpon it!

Easy Tip: There are many different Social Bookmarking services around the Internet. I have listed three of the major ones above. But, if you would like one button that takes care of virtually every Social Bookmarking service. Then the button from AddThis.com is excellent, which looks like this...

Then when someone hovers their mouse over the button, it expands into this...

Then the user can select their favorite Social Bookmarking service. It's a fantastic free service, and it only takes a quick copy and paste of the code that looks like this...

```
<!-- AddThis Bookmark Button BEGIN -->
<script type="text/javascript">
addthis_url = location.href;
addthis_title = document.title;
</script><script type="text/javascript"
src="http://s7.addthis.com/js/addthis_widget.php?v=12" ></script>
<!-- AddThis Bookmark Button END -->
```

So why talk about the other buttons individually when one button can do it all. Well, sometimes you want to steer the person bookmarking to a particular service to gain popularity with that service, so you only want to put up one or two buttons. But for many people, they just want to cover it all with one button; so AddThis.com works perfect!

Yahoo Directory Listing

YAHOO!. DIRECTORY Being listed in the Yahoo directory is excellent because it means an employee at Yahoo has come to your website, reviewed it and properly categorized it within the Yahoo directory. This means you have an actual link coming from Yahoo to your website. This is different than being listed in the Yahoo database search results.

This means there is an actual page on Yahoo that has a link to your website. Specifically, for us, that page is located at http://dir.yahoo.com/Business_and_Economy/Shopping_and_Services/Books/Bookstores/Computers/Internet/Titles/Business/

Both Yahoo and Google place significant importance on this link in boosting your search engine rankings because it means an actual human has reviewed your site and properly categorized it. It is well worth the $299 a year.

To be listed, just go to dir.yahoo.com and click on "suggest a site" and then on "get started." It asks some basic questions about your website, like the URL, title of the website and a description of the website. That's all you need and within seven days, a Yahoo employee will review your website, properly categorize it and place a link from Yahoo.com to your website.

This is a very helpful link to have and I highly recommend it!

PRWeb and Majon Press Releases

 Another excellent way to gain a high-quality keyword targeted link to your website is by using one or both of these press release companies to put out a Press Release for your business.

Sometimes, people feel that they have to have a major event to put out a press release. But that's not true. You can quite literally talk about anything you'd like to announce. However, if you have a remarkable aspect to your website, that's the best way to approach a press release and talk about it.

As an example, when I finished the BestWebsite Essential 9™, we released a press release for it through both of these companies. Within a few days, there were literally more than a hundred different websites linking to BestWebsite.com because of their great distribution network.

To me, only a few of them were high quality links. For instance, the actual press release posted on PRWeb.com and Majon.com are both high-quality links and there were a number of bloggers that chose to remark on the Essential 9 and the Canadian post even wrote a small blurb about it.

And biggest of all so far, Yahoo! News chose to distribute it through their news network. Even if we'd only gotten the two links from PR web.com and Majon.com, it's still worth the money. If you have something remarkable enough, then you'll get plenty of additional buzz, links and traffic to your website from others talking about you.

As an example, you can see our PRWeb.com press releases by going to their website and typing in BestWebsite.com or go directly here to see our first Press Release <u>prweb.com/releases/2007/10/prweb562862.htm</u>

If you're only going to use one service, I recommend PRWeb.com. I feel they provide the best value and the best distribution.

Links from Purchased Advertising

Last, but certainly not least, purchase advertising from websites within your industry that link to you. This is done last because by doing the other easy, mostly free, links first provides a much bigger bang for your buck because you've already created momentum for your search rankings.

The easiest way to go about this is just to type in the keywords for your market and see which websites rank on the first few pages. To me, it's not that important if you purchase advertising from a website that ranks either on the first or second page of the search results. They are always changing position anyway so it doesn't make much difference. You'll still get counted for a high-quality link.

As a clarification example, if you are running the Los Angeles photography website and you get a link from another website that ranks on the first page or two for the keyword Los Angeles photographer, from my perspective, this is still a high-quality link even if that particular website doesn't rank well with Alexa.com. The reason is because it is a link from a website within your market.

As far as what type of advertising to purchase, a text link, banner ad or display ad on their homepage is the best option, but also the most expensive. Any type of link from them pointing to you is very good. Also, keep in mind that the more the page the link is from deals with your market the better. The search engines know what the linked page is about and it counts better for you if it's relevant to your market.

> **Tip:** If you want to see what Google thinks your page is about, just copy and paste the Google AdSense code (google.com/adsense) onto one of your pages and look at the ads that Google displays next to it.

You can see below the BestWebsite Essential 9 page and the ads running next to it all deal with keyword research and Internet marketing. Perfect! This means Google understands what my page is about.

ng.. This is a great way to
in the world to your
website, categorizes it and
Google check if you have
ings. (1hr, $299/yr)

lajon.. This is a fantastic
ase, that are posted on their
yours. Not only do they
ankings, they also announce
3-5hrs, $308)

tising.. Find top websites in
n them. This may be one of
affic. Not only do you get
but they also drastically
use important websites in
. $100 and up)

rch Submit.. The more the
Don't make them guess. By
on your web pages and
ubmit. You let them gain
d in turn, they will rank you

68 hours, $1,266
110 hours, $3,466+

nt each of these, as well as other
e *Best Website* Book.

mmended businesses.)

Ads by Google

Search engine tips
Get your free business listing and get more web traffic. Free!
www.MerchantCircle.co

Truely Free Money Tools
Make money online - free info membeship site with no dues!
www.seoguidelite.com/

Increase Web Traffic Now
Advertise & Publish PPC - Earn Now Contextual Ad Matching w/ inContext
www.sellandtelladnetwc

Need Website Traffic?
Your Site Seen by Millions. Submit to Thousands of Free Sites!
www.megawebpromotic

So what is this chapter really about??

This chapter describes how to create high quality links for your website very quickly that not only boost search engine rankings, but can create significant traffic and exposure from the websites where you gained the link.

The reason I've recommended these seven websites is because you have control over getting them, you can get them very quickly, they are all high-quality links, and most of them are free!

It doesn't really matter when you're reading this book. Just take a look at the popular websites out there and figure out which ones you can get a link from and go after them.

If we're trying to rank well for a keyword like "Los Angeles photographer," I will likely need only two or three of these high quality links, plus the search engine optimization done to the website itself that targets this keyword, to achieve a first page ranking.

However, if you're like me and trying to rank well for a keyword like "search engine optimization," you will likely need all of these links, plus a lot of help from other websites deciding to link to you to achieve a first page ranking. This is why you will need to go after laser targeted keywords first ... ;o)

Most people will be able to achieve first page rankings with laser targeted keywords just from the links talked about in this chapter and doing the search engine optimization to your website talked about in the previous chapter.

Just keep adding the links until you get the rankings you're looking for. Many times, it will take a few weeks for your rankings to be boosted by the latest link you've added. Also, keep in mind that the longer your website is up, the higher it will rank.

Don't be intimidated, Get Started on Squidoo. Go On, Get Your Feet Wet!!

Written by **Amber Massey**, Vice President, BestWebsite® LLC

If you are a complete novice to the world of e-business, I highly recommend creating a lens on Squidoo.com. Why? First of all, because it is free. Second, because it is extremely user-friendly with great step-by-step instructions. Third, you get to give back to others by donating all or a portion of your proceeds from the Google Ads on your lens to the charity of your choice. And, perhaps most importantly, because building a lens will expose you to a lot of the same thought processes that you will need in order to build your own successful online business. THANKS, SQUIDOO!

The Skinny on Squidoo aka Squidoo Basics

Squidoo really did make itself extremely easy to use for everyone; the Internet expert, the novice and anyone in between is eligible to create a lens. What is a lens, you ask? A lens is a web page that you create on any topic you can think of that is hosted on Squidoo.com. Seth Godin, a legend in the Internet marketing community, is also the creative visionary who launched Squidoo. You can read his thoughts on creating a lens at http://www.squidoo.com/whybuildalens.

Once you arrive at Squidoo.com, you can either check out the Top 100 lenses http://www.squidoo.com/browse/top_lenses for inspiration, or you can boldly decide to Make Your Own

Lens http://www.squidoo.com/wizard/start right away and begin by completing the account creation process. It's quite simple. Then, you just pick a name for your lens and you are ready to start creating your lens. Squidoo requires at least 4 modules to be a finished lens, but no worries. Squidoo has provided its users with a long list of module choices that are great short-cuts to help you in designing an informative and unique lens on your topic. You can choose from basic text modules, to Amazon.com modules (that help you sell prod- ucts via your lens), to adding an RSS feed on the topic of your choice. The great thing about Squidoo is it is really all about you and what you want to communicate to others about your chosen topic.

9 Key Steps to Creating Your Best Lens on Squidoo:

1. Create a Squidoo Account.

2. Choose a topic for your lens.

3. Pick a charity and decide what portion of your pro- ceeds to donate.

4. Write your introduction module. To add pizzazz to your text modules, be sure to check out this great tutorial on html code that is targeted specifically to Squidoo, http://www.squidoo.com/basichtml.

5. Select Modules. Explore the modules that are available and choose those that best expand on your chosen topic. Modules help you customize your lens and Squi- doo makes it easy by constantly updating the module choices to expand your options and take advantage of the latest Internet technologies.

6. Personalize your lens by including a GuestBook module to allow visitors to provide feedback on your site and share their thoughts on your topic.

7. Be sure to add plenty of Tags (key words related to your lens topic) to help people find your lens.

8. Publish your lens for all the world to see. Be sure to let the world know about your Lenses, using email, joining Squidoo Groups, or social networking sites, such as Digg and Del.icio.us.

9. Update your Lens on a Regular basis. Squidoo likes fresh content, so continue to be innovative with your lens by updating with new modules. A great lens left untouched for a period of time will quickly drop in the lens rankings!

Don't stop with just one lens. Be sure to create more lenses on new or related topics and make each lens remarkable in its own right. Remember, Squidoo lenses are free to create, so feel free to share your knowledge and interests with the world.

Additional information about Squidoo, provided by Wikipedia

Squidoo is a website launched in October 2005 by Squidoo. com, LLC, based in Irvington, New York. It is a platform designed to make it easy for anyone, for free, to set up a single page on a topic he or she knows or cares a lot about. Squidoo came out of beta testing in March 2006.

Squidoo is a network of user-generated lenses – single pages that highlight one person's point of view, recommendations, or expertise. Lenses can be about anything, such as ideas, people or places, hobbies and sports, pets or products, philosophy, and politics. Lenses aren't primarily intended to hold content; more emphasis is placed on recommending and then pointing to content on the web. Annotation, organization and personalization deliver context and meaning.

Users who create lenses are called lensmasters. A lensmaster uses the tools available online to provide links, feeds, abstracts, and lists to users who are trying to make sense of a topic. For example, a single lens could point to Flickr photos, Google maps, blogs, eBay auctions, YouTube videos, and other links. Lensmasters are encouraged to promote personal agendas, expertise, causes, products, and opinions.

Squidoo splits its revenue with its "co-op" of lensmasters. Five percent goes straight to charity first. Then, 50% goes to the lensmasters and 45% goes to Squidoo. The site is estimating that nearly half of all the lensmasters are donating their royalties to any of 65 featured charities, ranging from NPR and The American Heart Association to smaller organizations like Chimp Haven and Planet Gumbo.

Squidoo was founded by author, speaker, and notable blogger, Seth Godin. On Godin's founding team were his book editor Megan Casey, and Fast Company employees, Heath Row, Corey Brown, and Gil Hildebrand, Jr.

According to Alexa, Squidoo's traffic has grown more than 40% monthly beginning in the spring of 2007. It is now in the top 500 of all websites tracked worldwide.

CH. 8 Make $100,000+ From Something You Already Have!

One of the easiest ways to make money online, no one talks about. I have made hundreds of thousands of dollars doing this and it's so simple it might surprise you. And at first glance, you might think it would be the last thing you want to do.

So what am I talking about?

Well, it starts with a story. In the year 2000, I was running a web design company called Blue Aspen Web Design. The business was doing fine and I had a number of steady clients. The only problem was I wasn't making a lot of money.

It took me quite a while to develop a website that turned people browsing my website looking for web design services into people who actually purchased design services from me.

So, about a year into running the web design business, I got the idea to sell a duplicate of my website, but change the name of the business, build it at a new domain name and change the contact information over to the new people that wanted to run their own web design business. This meant they didn't have to go through the entire process of setting up a successful business system themselves. Essentially, I would be selling a proven website business system.

This meant they could start out on day one with a ready made and tested website that was proven to convert browsers into buyers. I also included a short "How To" manual about how to run a successful web design business, even if they didn't know design themselves. I showed them how to hire out design work, get traffic to their site, how to close deals and price out design work.

It was only eight or nine pages and it highlighted my experiences in running my own successful web design business. That, coupled with the fact that they got a customized website with their business name and showing their picture as president and their contact information, was very valuable to a lot of people.

I sold more than 86 web design duplicate businesses to people wanting to run a web design company in about a year and a half. So here is where the interesting part starts to come in. If you are building a duplicate of a website that already exists, it only takes a fraction of the time it takes to build the original business.

As an example, it took me only 30 minutes to build an entire duplicate of a web design business complete with the new owners' business name and contact information. I was selling them for about $600 apiece. And, since as a web designer, I was only being paid $60/hr., I was more than happy to sell and build duplicates on the side for $1,200/hr.

(You can see the ad I used to sell the duplicates at BestWebsite.com/Bonus)

Okay, okay, I can hear some questions coming up so let me address them now. **Those are: 1.)** If you sell duplicates, aren't you hurting your original business? **2.)** Don't you have to be a web designer to pull something like that off? **3.)** Did the people buying the business understand they were getting a duplicate? **4.)** You said you made hundreds of thousands of dollars and that is only around $67,000?

Aren't you hurting your original business by selling duplicates? This is an interesting question and probably the biggest concern; if you are currently running a successful website, why would you want to dilute your market?

For the web design business, selling duplicates was not a problem because there were so many potential clients and only a handful of clients will keep their web design business doing very well.

Also, as I show later, it doesn't matter what kind of Internet business it is, selling duplicates can actually substantially help your website. As an example, you can build links back to your original website from all the duplicates, vastly increasing your search rankings within the search engines.

Don't you have to be a web designer to pull something like that off? Absolutely not, if you can use Microsoft Word, you can build duplicates of your site in no time. There are no inherently difficult tasks in building a duplicate. As an example, I'd like to go over the process of exactly how I built a duplicate website.

I opened up my website using Microsoft Expression Web, then I clicked File, then selected Published Web and typed in the new domain name of the web server I was publishing all the files to and clicked Publish. Expression Web then took every file on the original server and duplicated them to the new server so I had an exact copy. Expression Web is great because it updates all the hyperlinks within the new site to reflect the new domain name.

Next, I used the Find and Replace command to replace the old business name with the new business name. I did this for my personal name as well so it would show the new owner's name as President. Then, last, I opened the main header graphic at the top of each page displaying the business name, changed it over to the new business name and then dragged and dropped the new file into the /images/ folder of the new website, which automatically replaced the old one.

That's it, it just took me thirty minutes to earn $600.

Did the people buying the business understand they were getting a duplicate? Yes, what they were purchasing was well documented in the advertisement.

You said you made hundreds of thousands of dollars and that is only around $67,000? You're right, the web design duplicates were really just the beginning. When I realized that after I built a successful website business, it could be sold as a "duplicate" over and over again and that I could earn thousands of dollars, I definitely wanted to do it again!

So, after I sold the original web design business, I wanted to start something new. That's when I got the idea to start BuySellWebsite.com, which is a classified ad marketplace to buy and sell website businesses.

I remember when I first saw BizBuySell.com, the Internet's largest classified ad marketplace and thought – I can do that! It didn't look too hard, but I was very wrong. It took me almost two years of barely scraping by until it finally became consistent and started to grow on its own. I hope to show you how to do things much, much faster than I did.

By the second year, I had built the business into something reasonably successful at about $2,500 a month in profit. That's not very impressive I know, but it was profitable, nonetheless, and I could count on it every month.

So, here I was making about $30,000 a year and trying to find a way to make a lot more money. I decided to sell some duplicates of the original website into other markets when I realized Yahoo and Google were opening country-specific search engines. Instead of just Yahoo.com and Google.com, there is now Yahoo.co.uk and Google.co.uk that are built specifically for the United Kingdom market, giving local news, weather and search engine results for websites located in that country. You had to target those search engines to get into that market. **It now made sense to have separate websites to target them.**

So, I wrote a four paragraph advertisement and ran it on my own site BuySellWebsite.com (the original ad is below) since people coming to my site were already looking to buy a website business.

The response was phenomenal! I had no trouble selling the duplicates for $10,000 or more apiece. It still took the same amount of time to build, about thirty minutes, but now I was making ten thousand dollars for thirty minutes of work!

Yahoo has more than 28 country-specific search engines, targeting the United Kingdom, Australia, Japan, Canada, Mexico, India, France, Germany, Italy, Russia and Switzerland, among others. Each of these countries could be sold, totaling some $280,000.

> **Tip:** You can see Yahoo's complete country list by going to BestWebsite.com/bonus/ http://dir.yahoo. com/Regional/Web Directories/Yahoo International/

Since some of the duplicates I sold were not to English-speaking countries, the person I sold them to was responsible for translating the website themselves, that way other languages proved not to be a problem. I've even sold duplicates from people contacting me that wanted to run their own classified ad marketplace where no country-specific search engines existed, like in Peru and Denmark. They can really be sold to any country and any language.

Brief Recap: I originally had a website making $30,000 a year, but I was also, on average, selling one duplicate a month. It takes about a month to sell one because I had to run the ad, take questions about the business, agree on a contract, transfer money, have them set up the new web server, and then build the site.

> **Tip:** I chose to run one ad and then completely deliver the new site before I sold another one, but you could leave the ad up and sell them as fast as you can.

It was easy work and I was able to go from $30K a year to over $150K a year, almost overnight, all with a website that, at the time, was earning only $2,500 a month in profit.

There are many of these types of websites out there that a lot more can be earned from using this method. You don't even have to build your own; you can buy one that is already making money. See the Buying and Selling a Website Chapter.

I thought of another way to make money with this idea almost immediately. I didn't allow adult websites to be listed on my marketplace, so I built one exclusively for an adult classified marketplace. I was able to get the same $10,000 for each duplicate and quickly realized I could sell them to all 28 country-specific markets; consequently, I just added another $280,000 that could be earned from this business.

I was beginning to realize what an incredible way this was to earn money from an already existing website. I wanted to know how much I could sell the duplicates for. Was asking $100,000 possible? The answer was Yes!

If I put together a short Business Plan along with the website, showing how the marketing was done, how the website was built and financial projections, I could ask for and receive $100,000 for a single website duplicate! Wow!

The interesting thing is that the more money I was asking for, the easier they were to sell. I think this is due to the fact that the people with that kind of money to invest ask smart questions and can make a yes or no decision fairly quickly, making the selling process faster and you don't have to deal with as many people.

I have truly enjoyed this aspect of making money online. And I really love the thrill of building a new business and making it successful and, as a bonus, being able to make a lot more money from the business by selling duplicates.

It's a win-win for everyone. I'm creating businesses that provide value to people who purchase a product or service from me and I'm also able to sell duplicates so other people can earn money from their own business and provide a great product.

Tip: I give examples of Ads I ran to sell the duplicates later in this chapter and I show examples of the actual contracts I used in the BestWebsite.com/Bonus section.

Notes: To sell duplicates in the $100,000 dollar range, you definitely need to have a great website to start with to duplicate and a good believable business plan to go along with it that convinces the buyer your "duplicate" is fantastic. This sounds like a lot of work and it can be, but making $100,000 in a single day makes it well worth it!

I spend the majority of this book focusing on how to build a successful website to begin with because, without that, the selling of duplicates is not possible. There are really two ways to do it. The first is to build your own and the second is to buy an already successful website.

It is my recommendation that you build your own successful website business because, along the way, you'll learn all you need to know about running a website business. You will also have all the tools necessary to be able to sell duplicates because you'll have an understanding of all the details it takes to run a website business so that anyone reading your advertisements about buying a duplicate will have no doubt you know what you are talking about and will happily send you $10,000 or even $100,000.

People can easily see through your advertisements if you're not completely behind the project you are selling. When you are enthusiastic about it, knowledgeable about it and credible, this all shines through the words you write. The ad you write to sell it doesn't need to be lengthy, sometimes only three or four paragraphs – that's all you need to convey your message. Here are a few examples of ads I ran to sell the duplicates:

Original ad I ran for the United Kingdom duplicate (Ad #1) with an asking price of $10,000

Hello, my name is Nelson Bates and I own the site you are on right now (BuySellWebsite.com). I am looking for one person to help me launch the United Kingdom marketplace with a website that will be exactly like BuySellWebsite.com but will be modified to fit the United Kingdom market. I expect the business to generate $2,000 to $3,000 a month in net income within the first three to four months.

I will build the site and provide all the proven marketing knowledge I've learned over the last three years that has made the US version so successful. This includes keywords and phrases and promotional graphics as well as proper locations to advertise. The marketing strategy has been extremely well tested.

The site should take around 10-12 hours a week to run effectively. The database runs almost everything automatically - including accepting payments, taking the listings information from them, placing the ad automatically, rotating the ads properly and deleting the old ones. It also tracks the statistics for each ad and allows them to login to modify their listing at any time.

I've spent a lot of time making it automated and it works very smoothly. One of my Website Appraisers can complete the appraisals for you so you don't have to worry about learning that aspect. You keep a substantial amount of each appraisal purchased. I've also written an Operations Manual for the business that details exactly how the site is run so there is no confusion. Please contact me and I can send it to you via email in a PDF file.

The UK market is very big and has little competition so I'm looking forward to being #1 in the market as I've done here in the US. And, by the way, if you live in the UK, USA or anywhere else, it isn't a problem to run the site.

The purchaser of the UK Duplicate Rights will have full ownership of the site, however, once the entire investment has been earned back to the purchaser I will retain 10% of net income paid monthly. I will support the site for as long as you need me :o)

Here is another ad I ran. (Ad #2) with an asking price of $10,000

Hello, my name is Nelson Bates and I own the website you are on right now (BuySellWebsite.com) We are expanding our global reach and I'm looking for individuals to partner with to open up new international markets.

The remaining major markets I will be opening are: France, Germany, Italy, and Japan. There are also some slightly smaller markets, like Austria, Finland, and the Netherlands. These are all attractive markets for two reasons. First, they all accept either the EURO or the YEN currency and both of these are supported by PayPal which makes accepting international currencies very easy. And, secondly, all of these markets are served by Google and Yahoo Pay-Per-Click Advertising.

This allows us to enter the market quickly with a trusted advertiser that works with most major search engines in each country. These websites should make between $1,500 to $2,000 a month in Net Profit and take around 8 to 10 hours a week to run. Your main goal as the business owner will be to find additional places to advertise the website and build partnerships with other complementary businesses in the country. I will build the entire website for you (it's about 100 pages). You will be getting an almost exact copy of BuySellWebsite.com except it will be customized for the country you select.

You will also get all the keywords I've spent years researching to find the best and most profitable ones to launch your Pay-Per-Click campaign. And you'll get a proven banner ad to run, as well as my support as long as you need it.

You will need to have a reasonable understanding and comprehension of the country's language to be able to run the business effectively. Partners will own 90% of the business with 10% of income to be paid to BuySellWebsite for continued support.

Questions and Answers

Where can you run ads to sell duplicates?

I've found two great marketplaces to sell both duplicates and existing websites – one I built myself at BuySellWebsite.com and the other is BizBuySell.com. With a single ad placed on either of these marketplaces, you can expect to have more than 2,000 people click and view your listing. As a third option, there is BusinessesForSale.com but they are not as big.

How long was the average Business Plan you wrote?

I only needed eight pages to explain the target market, list the specifications of the website they were buying, outline the marketing campaign and give financial projections.

How much support did you have to give to the duplicates sold?

In general, I gave 90 days of support, which included phone and emails. The vast majority of people will want to be on their own as soon as possible and will not hound you. Most people will be on their own within two weeks. Don't be afraid to include support; it is one of the most valuable things you can include.

CH. 9 Buying and Selling A Website.

This is a topic I know a lot about. Not only did I see millions of dollars worth of Internet businesses being bought and sold each year on my website BuySellWebsite.com (I have since sold this business). But I have also personally sold hundreds of thousands of dollars worth of Internet businesses. Here's what I've learned …

If you have never run an Internet business before and you want to buy an already successful website to run, please note that most people who do it this way are only briefly able to maintain what the website was earning before they purchased it. And then, profits begin to drop rather quickly within three to six months.

What makes it really hard to do is there are so many little things you learn along the way in building your own website, as opposed to taking over an already successful one. Most new owners find it very difficult to update their new website and it becomes stale; if you pay someone else to do it for you, the costs quickly spiral out of control.

This is not to say you shouldn't do it. Just understand what you're getting yourself into. And if you follow the tips I now provide, you'll have the best shot possible of purchasing an already successful website. Right from the start!

Buying a Successful Website

To me, there are two great places to find successful websites for sale. Those are BuySellWebsite.com and BizBuySell.com. Both places consistently list currently operating and profitable websites for sale.

The best type of website you can buy is a website that delivers the product completely online ... Things like: membership sites, classified ad sites, websites where the revenue is made from advertising or anything else that is delivered online without your involvement.

Each situation is unique but, in general, it is my opinion that a website is essentially worth 1 to 1.5 times the yearly net income (profit) of the website. In other words, if the website earned $50,000 in profit last year, then that website is worth $50,000 to $75,000 on the open market.

Meaning, if you purchased the website for $50,000, you could earn your money back in a year if the website performed exactly the same as it did the year before.

So, here are some key questions to ask if you are interested in purchasing an Internet business.

1. Ask if you can login live to their PayPal account, 2Checkout.com account or other online credit card processing account so you can verify the sales made by their website.

Virtually all credit card processing accounts, including PayPal and 2Checkout.com, allow you to create a restricted login so people can view the payment history of the account, but are not able to change anything else. Ask the owner to create a restricted account like this so you can login.

Most owners of websites will <u>not</u> do this. The reason is because the financial numbers they have stated that the business is earning are either false or overinflated and you can quickly move on.

You will, however, encounter legitimate owners that will not allow a live login because they still feel it is a security risk. That's okay; ask them to print off the last three months of transactions directly from their credit card processor and fax them to you.

At that point you'll also need to verify bank statements from them and correlate them with the earnings shown via the credit card processing statements. If you continue to get evasive answers regarding the verification of the sales and expenses of the website, which you most likely will, then you'll know you need to move on to another website for sale.

2. If you have been able to verify payments to the website satisfactorily, it's time to ask how they built the website, meaning what software and coding was used to build the website. This will most likely be Adobe Dreamweaver or Microsoft Expression Web (formally Microsoft FrontPage).

Although you can use either software tool to modify a website built in either one, you really need to be an experienced web master to make this transition successfully. Otherwise, you'll need to purchase the web design software that the website was originally built in so you'll be able to make changes yourself.

To me, these are the two key elements to purchasing an already successful website, and being able to grow and build on that success and not have the website die on you.

If you can verify the income and expenses and you can modify the website yourself and then follow the promotional advice in this book, you should be well poised to grow and run your own profitable website business.

> **Notes:** Many website owners are not prepared for the grueling process that it takes to sell a website business. The website owner that you are dealing with has likely fielded many questions from many different potential buyers and is probably becoming frustrated with the process.
>
> The owner has also likely not properly documented his or her website financial earnings. This turns off many potential buyers. If you can add up some numbers by logging into their credit card processing account and looking at their bank statements, then sometimes you can come away with a fantastic deal because you can see the true value.

I have included in the bonus section (BestWebsite.com/Bonus) a Buy and Sell Agreement that you can use to either purchase a website or sell a website. In most of the transactions involving the purchase of a business, either one or both parties has never been through the process before, which complicates things.

Let me go over a typical transaction, and how it should take place …

After you have found a website you like and verified its expenses and earnings, you're now ready to begin the transfer process of your payment to the seller and the seller's assets transfer to you.

Unless it is a small amount of money, the transfer process should likely be a multistep process. In the Agreement the transfer process should be spelled out something like this ...

> After buyer pays seller a deposit of $2,500 through PayPal.com, the seller will remove the business for sale from the market and transfer one of the two domain names included in the sale to the buyer. Then, after a wire transfer of $25,000, the seller will transfer the main domain name to the buyer as well as transfer the web hosting account, and email newsletter list to complete the initial transaction. Seller also agrees to 90 days of support.

There are multiple reasons to do it this way. It allows the buyer to put up some money and get at least one asset, in this case, a second domain name that is included with the sale. Also, if you make payment through PayPal, you can get your money back if something should go wrong. However, if you do it all through wire transfer, you have to sue to get your money back should something go wrong.

Tip: You can make payment entirely through PayPal. com or other credit card processor; however, most sellers don't want to do this because of the credit card processing fees charged.

As a buyer, you have to take some things on faith and trust the seller. If you find any reason not to trust the seller, then it's probably best to move on.

The bonus section does a good job of giving a full example of an Agreement in Microsoft Word format you can download and modify as you please. It looks something like this ...

Buy Sell Agreement for YourName.com

Date:

1. Names

2. Assets included in agreement

3. Specifics of transfer

4. Total purchase price

5. Deposit

6. Payment at Closing

7. Debts and outstanding accounts

At the time of closing, Seller states that there are no debts on the assets or outstanding accounts. The Seller has paid all known debts and other liabilities of the businesses in the partnership.

8. Seller Representations

Seller represent(s) and warrant(s) that:

[ ] A. Seller owns the assets being sold. At closing, the assets will be free from any claims of others.

[ ] C. Seller is (and at closing will be) a limited liability company in good standing under the laws of the state of … , and has (and at closing will have) the authority to perform the obligations contained in this sales agreement.

[ ] D. The total liability of Seller for all breaches of representations and warranties will not exceed $20,000.

9 Buyer Representations

Partner 2 represents and warrants that:

[ ] A. Buyer has inspected the assets that he is purchasing, and has carefully reviewed Seller's representations regarding them. He is satisfied with the assets.

[ ] C. Buyer is (and at closing will be a sole proprietor in good standing under the laws of the state of ... , and has (and at closing will have) the authority to perform the obligations contained in this sales agreement.

[ ] E. Buyer will indemnify, defend, and hold Seller harmless from and against any financial loss, legal liability, damage, or expense arising from any breach of the above representations and warranties.

[ ] F. The total liability of the Buyer for all breaches of representations and warranties will not exceed $20,000.

10. Closing

The closing will take place:

Date: September 12th 2008

Time: 12:00 Noon

[ ] 11. Disputes

If a dispute arises concerning this agreement or the sale, Seller and Buyer will try in good faith to settle it themselves. If no satisfactory settlement is arrived upon after 30 days, Buyer and Seller will enter mediation conducted by a mediator to be mutually selected.

Seller and Buyer will share the cost of the mediator equally. Seller and Buyer will cooperate fully with the mediator and will attempt to reach a mutually satisfactory resolution of the dispute.

If the dispute is still not resolved within 60 days after it is referred to the mediator, Seller and Buyer agree that the dispute will be arbitrated by an arbitrator to be mutually selected. Costs of arbitration, including lawyers' fees, will be allocated by the arbitrator.

12. Risk of Loss

Seller will replace or pay for the replacement of any assets that are destroyed or damaged before the closing.

13. Entire Agreement

This is the entire agreement between the parties. It replaces and supersedes any oral agreements between the parties, as well as any prior writings.

14. Modification

This agreement may be modified only by a written amendment signed by both parties. Electronic signatures are acceptable.

15. Governing Law

This agreement will be governed by and interpreted under the laws of the state of ... , and any litigation will be brought in the courts of that state.

16. Severability

If a court or arbitrator determines that a provision in this agreement is invalid or not enforceable, that determination will affect only that provision. The provision will be modified only to the extent needed to make it valid and enforceable. The rest of the agreement will be unaffected.

17. Notices

All notices must be sent in writing. A notice may be delivered to a person at the address that follows the person's signature or to a new address that the person designates in writing. A notice may be delivered:

A. in person

B. by certified mail, or

C. by overnight courier.

Date:

Seller:

Signature_____

Buyer:

Signature_____

CH. 10 Interview with SEO Expert Jill Whalen of High Rankings®

Jill Whalen, CEO of Highrankings.com, is one of the most knowledgeable experts on search engine optimization in the world. I chose to interview her because of her extensive knowledge and clear understanding of this complex subject.

Jill's website has consistently ranked on the first page with the industry's most competitive keywords for more than a decade. Please read this valuable, exclusive interview with BestWebsite®.

1. Congratulations on HighRankings.com being the number one Search Engine Optimization site. What factors would you say had the greatest impact on your current success?

Thanks!

The factors that had the greatest impact on my success and that of High Rankings would be my overall love of SEO, and my dedication to the Search Marketing industry in general. I live, breathe, eat and sleep SEO, and I believe this comes out in everything that I do, whether it be in the free High Rankings Advisor newsletter, the High Rankings Forum or in the work we do for our clients.

Being authentic, open and honest about everything we do, and our mission of making the Internet a better place for all, seems to resonate with people.

2. What do you love most about SEO?

There's so much to love that it's hard to choose. But I guess it would be the whole puzzle aspect of it. Each site presents its own set of challenges and problems to figure out. Once you do figure it out, it's a great feeling. And it's even better when you see that your fixes actually worked! Because SEO is not an exact science, you never quite know if your fixes will work. Everything you do is based on experience and gut instinct. Thankfully, our fixes do indeed work nearly every time!

3. What pending changes in the SEO industry concern you the most?

Most of the changes in the SEO industry lately are actually good things, so I don't have too many concerns. If I had to choose, however, I'd say that the rebirth of some new SEO software is slightly concerning. Anyone who's done SEO for a few years knows that no software can do what needs to be done to fix a site so that it's the best it can be for search engines and people. That said, some SEO tools do have good features that can speed up the SEO consultant's job. My concern is more in relation to those tool companies that market their products as an alternative to hiring an SEO company.

4. Is hiring SEO services a good idea for everyone?

If you have more money than time, then yes. But SEO isn't rocket science, so if you have more time than money, you can certainly learn the basics and do it yourself. In fact, everything you need to know about doing SEO yourself is available for free at the High Rankings website!

5. What advice would you want website owners to consider or implement on their sites prior to seeking out SEO services?

The less they do first, the better because they may very likely do it wrong! We unfortunately see so many websites that design or redesign their websites and THEN hire an SEO agency. Since so much of SEO is in making sure the site has the appropriate navigation, this often has to be completely redone. All website owners contemplating a new website should also be consulting with an SEO at the same time.

6. What keyword tools do you use?

At High Rankings we generally use KeywordDiscovery these days. However, Wordtracker is also still good, as is Google's own keyword tools.

7. What is your selection criteria or process for choosing keywords?

We choose the keyword phrases that are the most relevant to the page at hand, as well as the most likely to get searched upon at the search engines.

8. Can you give us your top 5 strategies for improving SEO rankings for a new website?

* Keyword Research to ensure that you optimize for keyword phrases people are actually searching on at the search engines.

* Deciding what top-level and sub-level pages the website needs to have designed, based on the keyword research.

* Creating compelling Title tags that use the keyword phrases, while also appealing to a searcher who might find the listing in the search results pages at the engine. (Title tag info is what shows up as the clickable link to your site in the search results pages.)

* Having professionally written copy that utilizes the keyword phrases the page is optimized for, while also maintaining an emotional connection to the reader.

* Getting the word out about the website to other people, companies and websites who might be interested in what you're offering.

9. Would you recommend the same strategies for an existing online business struggling to maintain or grow traffic?

Yes, the SEO process is basically the same, except it will take a lot longer for a brand new website to see results, and more publicity will be needed to get the word out.

10. What other factors might an existing website need to consider?

Existing websites may want to review their current link profile to see if the best anchor text (the words in the clickable part of a link) is being used. If at all possible, it's helpful to have a keyword phrase as part of the anchor text. This can't always be changed, but it's possible that contacting some of the linking site owners, a deal can be made to have them changed.

11. What are some of the mistakes you've made in running your website?

The main mistake I've made with my website is not reviewing the copy on my services pages often enough so that they don't get out of date. It's funny how 2 or 3 years can sneak up on you, and service offerings can change a lot during that time period.

12. Are there revenue streams you wish you'd explored earlier?

Not that I can think of. Our major revenue stream is our services. We've made some additional money via affiliate links in the High Rankings Advisor newsletter for products that we recommend and use ourselves, plus our High Rankings Seminars were an additional stream. But, all in all, I'm happy with the various revenue streams we've explored through the years.

13. Where do you see yourself and your business one year from now?

Pretty much right where it is now! 2007 was a year of expansion for me. I no longer work at home by myself. I have an office, plus 2 additional employees. By the end of 2008, I may hire at least 1 other employee, perhaps even 2 if necessary.

14. Five years from now?

That is more difficult to say, because SEO changes frequently. The plan is to continue to grow High Rankings and hire a few new employees each year, so in 5 years, it would be realistic to assume we might have 10-12 employees.

15. What steps do you feel will help grow your business?

We've been taking lots of steps already this year. High Rankings is in the process of getting a new look, complete with new logo and branding. The website is being completely redesigned and should be launched before the end of the year. My hope is that the new branding will showcase High Rankings as the brand and less Jill Whalen as the brand. I'll of course continue to be a major part of the organization, but training others to do the day-to-day client work will be a big key in the growth process.

I'll be speaking at more events, doing more in-house training, and more article writing for offline and online publications. The goal is to become a thought-leader for the search marketing industry.

16. How do you balance your home and work life? Can a successful business woman really "have it all?"

I can't say that balance is my strong suit! As I mentioned, I live and breathe SEO, so I generally don't separate my work from my home life. I do go into the office every day now, so that does help to separate them somewhat. The good thing is that my kids are older and only my son is still at home. He's 14 and doesn't need any supervision, so if he's home alone a lot when I'm away, it's not that big of a deal. My husband is also a great help. He makes sure we get out by ourselves a few nights a week, so that I get away from my computer once in awhile!

Interview conducted by Amber Massey, Vice President, Best-Website, LLC

CH. 11 Feeling Frustrated? Overwhelmed??

Good!! That's what keeps my competition down, and that's the same thing that keeps your competition down. Starting an Internet business and building it into something that is profitable is incredibly difficult to do.

If you have never registered a domain name before, you will likely feel confused before you start, unsure of your options during the signup process and then after you've registered it, you'll feel like you've done something wrong.

The same thing is true with setting up your web server; you'll feel bewildered with the number of options, confused with the control panel and not sure how to log in with your web design software to start building your first page.

I'm now in my 12th year of making money online. More than six of those have been full-time and I still feel uncomfortable with many things. For instance, when I submitted my first Digg article, I experienced a moment of panic since I didn't know how the Digg community would react because they might ridicule me for submitting something that was considered stupid.

If you understand that being uncomfortable is part of the game, you're already ahead of the game because most people are waiting until they feel "comfortable" to start their Internet business.

I'm here telling you that you will never feel completely comfortable. It's just the nature of the business. There are few black and white answers, mostly answers somewhere in the middle.

To me, this book is remarkable by the fact of what's not talked about. There are so many different directions that appear to be correct when you are first starting out. By streamlining your efforts to the proven success strategies I've shared with you in this book, I hope to save you years of time with my extensive Internet business experience. And I hope to make you feel as comfortable as possible as you move forward into building your own profitable website.

Also, don't feel that because this book is out there, everyone now knows about the techniques. Even if the book is very successful, it's likely that only one or two of your competitors will know about it, much less will implement any of it.

I have a few different recommendations, depending on your situation …

If you have never started an Internet business before and you have an idea of what you'd like to sell and you've done some keyword research, then you're ready to register a domain name!

Go to GoDaddy.com and type in the domain name you'd like; if it's not available, they will make suggestions of names that are available. Select one that you like and go through the registration process. Remember, they'll try to sell you all kinds of add-ons along the way. Just say no to everything. Then point your DNS servers to Intermedia.net (Step by step instructions provided in Chapter 4).

If you're having difficulty with anything related to your domain name, call GoDaddy at 480-505-8877.

Then, go to Intermedia.net and sign-up for their Windows QuickWeb hosting account ($9/mo). After you've done these two things, most often, after a few hours you'll be able to log in using your web design software and create your first page on the Internet. Sometimes, it takes a day or more to setup though.

If you have Microsoft Expression Web and you've registered your domain name and set up your Web server, do this to get started. Start Expression Web, click "File," then "Open Site." Type in http://www.yourdomainname.com and click "Open"; it will then ask you for your Intermedia password; it will load the site and you'll be looking at the basic structure of your web server.

Double-click the file on the left titled, "welcome.htm," labeled 1.) below (it's the default page that is automatically created for you when you sign up), then in the right-hand panel the page will pop up for you to modify, delete the text, and type in ...

I'm on my way!

Then, click "File" and "Save"; go to a browser and type in your domain name and you'll see a blank page with the words you just typed.

> **I think at this point you'll see the power you now have because the ideas in your head can now be shared with the world!**

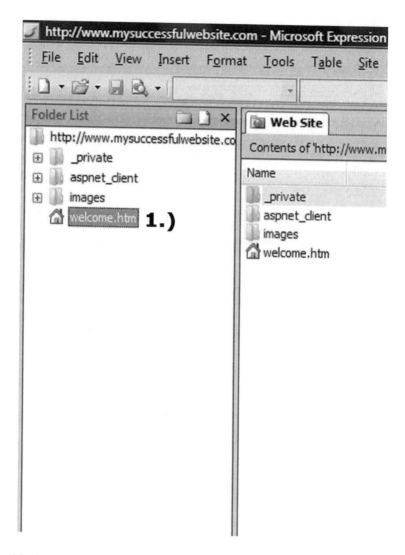

You're now ready to follow the rest of the advice in this book and be on your way to building a profitable Internet business of your own!

If you already have a website built but aren't making money or haven't made as much as you'd like, there are several things you can do. You likely don't have a remarkable aspect to your business and/or you don't have enough traffic to your website to convert into sales.

The advice in this book will be tremendously helpful to you because you've already experienced many of the issues you need to deal with when running an Internet business.

If you've read this far in the book, I'm sure you already have a good sense of what you need to do to make your website successful. The number one most important thing for any website is traffic because if you have enough traffic, you can even make up for having a poor, unremarkable website. Of course, you can make **much more money** if you have a remarkable website as well.

Good Luck!

Check BestWebsite.com/Bonus for free updates to this book.

Notes

Free Articles For Your Website, Newsletter or Blog

You are welcome to use the ready to go, copy and paste articles that come from the content of this book. It is a great way to get high-quality content, in easy copy and paste format.

Each "**Article 6-Pack**" contains six ready to go articles. You can use one or all in any order you choose.

Please visit **www.BestWebsite.com/FreeArticles** to get the text files.

Best Website® Educational Video Series

Check BestWebsite.com/video for our free Internet Marketing and eBusiness educational videos. A great way to learn about the techniques in the Best Website book, as well as a number of other strategies not covered in the book.

Partner with us

We have a number of excellent website business ventures available from $10,000-$100,000+ You can own a piece of Best Website® and earn hundreds of thousands of dollars running your own business! Please contact us for information!

Web Business Consulting

If you would like personal coaching to start, build or grow your Internet business, please visit our About Us section

(BestWebsite.com/about) to see the available consultants. Just mention you saw this ad in the book and receive 20% off.

Literary Agents:

If you are interested in representing the Author and Book Series **Best Website™** *Simple Steps to Successful Websites* - we will be happy to send you a complete marketing campaign for your review:

Business Development

Please contact us at **moreinfo@bestwebsite.com** or **800-681-4176** for any joint venture, cross promotion or advertising opportunities.

Acknowledgements

A HUGE thank you goes to Amber Massey. She did some un-believably excellent work editing, reworking and hashing over ideas for the book. I feel very lucky to have her a part of my team, and I'm grateful for her consistent hard work!

Certainly a big thank you also goes to my Mom and Dad who read a number of the early versions of the book and gave me valuable feedback. The same goes for Sarah Martini who let me use her photography website as a great example.

While I was nearing the completion of the book, I got a big boost of confidence from Seth Godin; ..who just by respond-ing to my e-mails made me feel like a million bucks!! To me, he is the smartest marketer I know, and I'm grateful he knows I exist..;o)

Also, Lauren Woolley and Tim McManus at BookSurge have been incredibly helpful. They have definitely made the publish-ing process easy and enjoyable!!..

I'd also like to thank Edit911.com for doing a fantastic job pro-fessionally editing the book! I certainly recommend them.

And if you've read this far, I'd like to thank YOU the reader. It's you who the book is for; to help you earn money, gain financial freedom, help others in the process, and enjoy the ride along the way!! Thank you very much for reading.

Nelson Bates, President

About the Author: Nelson Bates

Some of Nelson's history include; building the internet's most successful marketplace to buy and sell internet businesses (BuySellWebsite.com) This company was selected by the #1 internet marketing company in the world, The Internet Marketing Center® as a Featured Success Story. (Read Article at BestWebsite.com)

He also developed the Internet's longest running Website Appraisal ™ system and has worked as a Web Master for Walt Disney World®.

Nelson graduated from Kansas State University with a degree in Marketing.

To interview Nelson please e-mail nelson@bestwebsite.com or call 800.681.4176

2652742

Made in the USA